CW00853113

Manhandling,

Myths

& Mudholes

By Sara Jayne McLeod

A thought provoking, unashamedly honest, yet humorous commentary on Singlehood

Dr. Sara-Jayne McLeod

Manhandling, Myths and Mudholes

© 2020, Dr. Sara-Jayne McLeod

www.adammeetevehere.com

All rights reserved.
No part of this publication may be reproduced, stored in a retrieval system, stored in a database and / or published in any form or by any means, electronic, mechanical, photocopying, recording or otherwise, without the prior written permission of the publisher.

To my mother Carmen who is the lead heroine in my life

Contents

Foreword

Growing up in the Church, single women were told to wait on God! Could you imagine the many questions that they would have had about their Singlehood experience?

Sara breaks it all down! She has shared her story. The conversation you have had in your head is laid bare on these pages. There is no judgment here, and there are no lies here. She has cut through the pretence, the fear, and the unspoken and above all... the frustration! She has answered vital questions with guidance and beautifully chosen scriptures.

If you live in your head wondering if you are the only one going through a rollercoaster in Singlehood. If you are suffering from low self-esteem, doubt, confusion; this book is really for you.

I think it is time to call the Churches to take issue on. Praying for Singles is a start, but support needs to include practical solutions.

Sara has taken time to write this book and the truth is, it needed the time. This journey is a carefully documented daily experienced lived with hope and expectation, fear, disappointment, but not without hope!

You will find this book hard to put down. Never before have we heard this story told, the heart ultimately laid bate in a world where everyone is presenting their best self, no flaws, no mistakes, no worries, and just fooling the world. This book says, I'm just going to tell you my truth, and with great tips and guides, I hope it helps.

This will more than help its time to had this book out in Church and have this very real, overdue conversation that is hurting, women, and hurting our community. To all the Church leaders, This is your next book to read.

Thank you, Sara, for putting yourself out there, it was time. Gods Time.

Angie Le Mar

Preface

I would like to honour all the women in my life who have been my accountability hedge, past and present.

To my wonderful family who are anointed to put up with me.

To my amazing parents who have invested lovingly and sacrificed so much for my well being.

I want to make you proud. If there is anything honourable to be said about me... you are all responsible.

To the women who do not want to be single, this book is for you.

Introduction

Wow! Firstly, I did not think that anyone would be interested in hearing what little old me had to say. I am totally overwhelmed and grateful, but also nervous about my reputation. Even though God gave the green light; it took a lot of arguments with myself to release this book. I do not doubt for one second that some of the conservative folk who watched me grow up... might be in for a shock. Never the less, I wrote this book for YOU. I wrote it for every woman of God who has considered herself a hopeless romantic and yet romantically hopeless.

A woman who loves God, yet finds herself coasting from one heart-breaking situation to another. A woman who may have furiously flipped through the Bible, almost ripping pages, looking for the reason why she is not married yet. Each time she got played, she promised herself it was the last time. Not even a dog returns to its own vomit. Yet WE intelligent, kind-hearted, gifted ladies, find ourselves making the same mistakes; and are oh so shocked when we see the same results. Why? ...Well, we will certainly talk about it!

You may have, just like me, given up on the idea that there is a husband for you. For those who do not have children, you wonder whether you should start making some alternative arrangements? Between you and me, I had bookmarked some adoption websites online years ago. Can we keep it real? I understand all too well, the frustration that comes with being a Christian woman in the 21st century, living with the desire to love a great man.

I must warn you, if you are expecting this commentary to be delicate and cute, you will be sorely disappointed. I am fluent in Christianise, but that dialect is not appropriate for this topic.

I ask: How are you?
You: Blessed and highly favoured.

Not today! During the reading of this book, you will be challenged to remove any and all masks. Be honest with yourself because you do not have to impress anyone. Holiness is not demonstrated by suppressing your truth. God knows it all, and it is His desire that you walk in freedom. Let the real emotions surface and confront the whole truth of how you really feel being single.

Did you know you could be getting in the way of your own personal breakthrough? No more pretending. If you go to the doctors, you are unlikely to hide your symptoms or conceal how severe your condition is. This would prevent the doctor from making the correct diagnosis and managing your conditions appropriately. You are harming yourself in the long run. We are very good at masking our dysfunction, but understand there is a better way to live. I believe we should be as honest as possible. So tell it like it is.

On some days...

You may ask: How are you?

Me: I am doing better today, but yesterday I felt lonely and sexually frustrated. It was that bad, I thought I was going to jump the next guy that walked by.

Over here, we talk frankly, from porn to self-harm through to prayer and lust. I could not squeeze everything in-between these covers, but I hope it is enough to help somebody.

Although I have tried, I cannot separate my Christian faith from my love life. If Jesus is Lord of my life, then my belief in Him should influence my thoughts and choices in singlehood. I did not always feel this way, but my, did I make some foolish decisions? I soon found that the more Godly wisdom you arm yourself with, the smarter choices you will make with your heart.

So, sister girl, I encourage you to take your time while reading and prayerfully consider the things I am going to present to you. You may not agree with all of it, or even some it; but as long it starts some urgent love conversations, my job is done.

So Sara Jayne, who on earth are you? I was born in London; "multicultural and urban" is probably the most politically correct way to describe this English postcode. My family are active Christians, and that is that. I can honestly say I do not remember a time when I did not know God was real.

I was the stereotypical Pastors Kid.

> I know a little girl
> Who had a big curl
> Right in the middle of her
> forehead.
> When she was good
> She was very very good
> But when she was bad.
> She was horrid.
>
> Henry Wadsworth Longfellow

Two thumbs up. That was me. Times were not all bad ,but I was one of the moodiest "Emo" teenagers you could have imagined. I got away with a lot because I was good at school.

I suffered from depression secondary to being overweight, and I overate because I was obese (classic cycle of destruction.) I was the psycho sister who shouted at everyone when she was ready and used to watch herself cry in the mirror. But most of the time, I reckon I had a lot of fun, lived in my vivid imagination, and was a loud, friendly character.

I want to make this abundantly clear from the jump-off. I am 31 years old, and I have **NEVER** been in a relationship before. I did not go on my first date until 28 years old. I have not been idle though, oh no, I have been in plenty of situation-ships, and I have "hung out" with young men who did not know what to do with me. Oh, good times!

I learned about relationships likely the same way you may have. My own parents, TV, friends, music, school, church, Disney and the list goes on. I tried to make sense of it all came up with the idea that if you did not find love, you were not the right person. Beautiful, successful women have a distinct look, and they have a husband. Allow me to reference the blockbuster hit: 'Inception,' once those foolish ideas planted themselves in the deep recesses of my psyche, I could not shake it.

Have you ever struggled with low self-esteem but know in the back of your mind that there is greatness inside of you?

In my situation, it is embarrassing to be so academically astute but socially dumb. Psychologists reckon that there are at least ten different kinds of intelligence. Just because you are advanced in one area of your life, does not necessarily mean that you are accomplished in all areas.

I am happy to announce that God HAS transformed my life by renewing my mind. This book concludes with a celebration, so I wanted to share life lessons from my journey. I appreciate that an unmarried woman at 46 will have a different narrative on singlehood. But I also feel that I have reached a milestone. This is a great time to reflect on what God has done in me and for me. I want to address some of the taboos that are secretly keeping women like me bound with shame.

"Manhandling, Myths and Mudholes" chronicles matters that a woman must conquer to successfully guard her peace; and maintain her focus in her singlehood season. Whether marriage comes or not, she must become who God designed her to be.

Also, I want my sisters to know that they do not have to completely relinquish their desire for marriage to be that ideal Christian woman. You can be faithful and practical at the same time.

They always tell you to guard your heart, but they never give enough detail as to how and what from. How would I even recognise who to let down my guard for? I stumbled through this season until I accepted that there were blind spots in my knowledge about love, dating, and singleness. I have a medical background, and I finally started to use my diagnostic skills on myself. This was a process that contained elements that I did not enjoy. I had to filter my ideas about self-worth, love, and men.

I studied the Word, I talked to God a lot, read books, listened to sermons, and counselled with people far wiser than I. I listened to the Holy Spirit when He said that... had to change. As a result, my life has transformed for the better, and the first step was confronting the truth. You cannot fix what you cannot acknowledge.

Please do use this book as an aid to help you reflect on your own journey. Are you at peace with your singlehood? Are you being ghosted by potentials that break your heart? Are you going through a cycle of bad situations? Do you have some bad habits or issues managing your sexual nature? Do you desire to be closer to God and feel as if your love life is actually an area of hurt you cannot cross to get to him? Whatever it is you are facing, you are more than a conqueror through Christ. It is going to work OUT as we work WITH Him.

Chapter One

_____Manhandling_____

What I am about to say sounds counterintuitive: sometimes to move forward you have to look back. You read that correctly. I know what Apostle Paul said, forgetting those things that are behind, I press on towards the mark of the high calling of Christ Jesus our Lord. I completely agree that you cannot drive a car forward using the rearview mirror. However, what I am talking about is the essential learning from previous mistakes. If you do not make time to reflect on negative or traumatic experiences, you will not mature.

You can survive something and not mature from it. Maybe it was a situation that happened to you... you are not culpable. Have you ever acknowledged the impact it had on you? Have you confronted your feelings about it? Have you sought the right help to heal? Many are walking around with invisible scars and internal bleeding that only manifests when they want to love again. Maybe ugly words you heard changed the way you saw yourself for the worse. Perhaps you have not forgiven yourself for a mistake you made. Pretending that something that hurt you did not happen is not strength and positivity. The healthy woman understands that life will deal blows. Still, there is a victory in recovering and not getting knocked the same way again. (When it is in her control of course.)

The looking back is not about remaining in that moment. It is a focused exercise, where you reflect for learning. If you are always on the move... getting into situations... falling... popping back up... running somewhere new. You may miss patterns and the hidden lessons that will positively shape your character.

God took me on a journey not to condemn me but to heal me. He taught me not to be ashamed of my story. His grace shines through my flaws. I needed to accept some hard truths about myself, but also acknowledge where I was hurt. I needed to see my growth, which led me to accept myself for the wonderful woman He made me. I had to admit that I am working progress but also a masterpiece. It took me a while to stop equating my value to my marital status. There were a few steps to take to appreciate rather than loathe singlehood. The first step was to confront how I "handled men" and how I allowed them to "handle me."

Well… at the risk of my reputation hold out your cup. I got a little tea that might help you understand me a bit better. I have selected a FEW stories from my past that sadly reveal how immature and clueless I was. I do not write from an ivory tower looking down at anyone. I know all too well how to shut God out of your love life.

I am sorry to say that I carried on preaching and teaching even when I had not overcome my issues. The truth was I was a hypocrite and in danger of going to hell. I know I was walking in rebellion for a whole season. When I reflect, I do not understand why God was so patient with me. I thank Him daily for His grace and mercy. It was my constant confrontation with the Word and the Holy Spirit that eventually captured and delivered my soul.

Shall we get real? Yes, we shall.

Tea

Disclaimer: All the names and personal identifying information have been changed to maintain privacy.

Back in the days when MSN was relatively new, I got myself into a lot of trouble. The social media pages we used were "My Space" and "Hi5" We teenyboppers spent hours designing our pages using HTML code generators. I bet the young people do not even know what that is! It was fun, it was popular, and we used these platforms to meet people. Then you held proper instant messengers conversations on MSN... on a computer!! Goodness help you if you had restricted Internet access. To be honest, the ethernet cable you plugged was more reliable than intermittent wifi.

I took to social media like a duck to water. I displayed boldness online that I lacked in real life. It was all fun and games getting into guys' heads. Teasing them with cybersex and then laughing at their foolish responses over lunch the next day at school. We were free online, we could be whoever we wanted to be. And because no guy pursued me in "real" life, I lapped up the online attention like a thirsty dog at a stream in the Sahara desert.

BADGER

I remember one particular boy who charmed me. I wanted to drop all the other dudes I was talking to. The aim was to focus on making him my next online boyfriend. (By the way, I do not consider these situations to be relationships). Unfortunately, a persistent young man I will call Badger refused to get dropped. Badger kept texting and calling. His persistence was intriguing; plus the boy I really wanted, was playing hard to get. So I ended up entertaining the Badger. There was nothing spectacular about him;

sadly, he was not doing well at school. He had a good heart, but he was not who I needed to be talking to.

On the outside, I was doing all right, budding worship leader/speaker, good grades at school, but on the inside, I was messed up. There were some bad things I had gotten into that I will tell you about later. I was addicted to the attention. We did not have a relationship but a situation-ship. We did meet, and I compromised my integrity. He was my first kiss, and it was not pleasant. It was the closest I got to losing my virginity.

I stopped talking to him the very same evening I got home from our meet-up. The regret was immediate and shoved me headfirst into depression. Guilt consumed me and destroyed my self-esteem. He did not understand why I did not want to talk to him and even up to a year later tried to email me.... I did not know how to deal with it, so I ignored him.

The Curse

It took me about two years to fully recover from that low point because I really did want to live right. I messed up, and I did not know how to forgive myself despite repenting. Not too long after the slipping incident, I remember a particular Sunday service. The memory is in High Definition to this very day because this moment changed my life.

I was sitting in church as the service was in full flow. The morning speaker was doing his thing, and I sat there, finding it difficult to tune in. Suddenly, I heard a strange internal voice. **"You might as well become a lesbian because no good man would ever want you."** I can number on the one hand the amount of time the adversary has spoken to me directly. You guys can brush it off as deep fear surfacing, but this voice was alien. It did **NOT** come from me. That was all that it said. I started to cry silently in my seat as a poisonous seed was planted in my spirit and pushed way down. This seed was planted, and because no one knew it was there, it began to germinate, and I accepted this lie as a truth.

Has there been an early traumatic experience or awful things said to you that you have internalised? The Devil is smart; he will study you to find your weakness.

HOWEVER The Devil and God are not opposites, God created Lucifer as an archangel, and he fell. There was no Marvel comic battle in heaven. He got knocked out, and your God will always be in control. But understand that he does not fight fair. His plan is not to annoy you but to destroy your life. Watch out for the lies he tries to plant.

This lie masquerading as the truth would cause me to make some very foolish decisions to "break" the curse. Sigh. I am rolling my eyes as I write this because it sounds so silly. But that was my reality growing up. My personal life was pitiful and sad because I allowed spiritual weeds to grow. I let it morph into a giant oak, which choked out the seeds of life God had planted.

Think about the parable of the sower. Read about four different responses to hearing Gods' word in Matthew 13.

Living with that spiritual wound meant I was heading into the world with vulnerabilities and weaknesses, limiting success for any romantic relationship. Plus, I had the disadvantage of being overweight. I live in England, and in this culture, we do not celebrate or promote plus-sized women.

I have been overweight most of my life, and I have never accepted it. I feel like I am beautiful inside, but my outside appearance is disguised by layers of fat. Yes, bigger women have found men attracted to them, but this was not my experience. Guys are physical creatures, and most that I have met have struggled to see past my size. So I had this "curse*" on the one hand and the obesity on the other!! (*Just to be clear, I am not and have never been attracted to women. However, if homosexuality is your struggle, be encouraged that there is freedom from that soul issue.

God loves you as you are and know that I love you too.)

I seemingly "got over" the Badger Bonanza and was literally hungry for a relationship. I felt there must be someone in this big old world that wants me. Here comes the big girl, big personality, confident, talented, but hopelessly single. I was the agony aunt who gave so much advice to my friends who had boyfriends. I was that supporting actor in the middle of a drama holding the bags while action played in the foreground. Nothing was popping in my own life.

I found it so much easier to pray and ask God for anything. I had no significant problems regarding my career, family, ministry, community, the world, even my own health (at the time). But when it came to my social life, it was a cemetery. I was finished. Everything I had gone through had pushed me over the edge. I lost all confidence in myself as a woman. I saw myself as a spiritual drone, built to minister and bless people. I had abilities as a medical doctor, but as a woman, I was worth nothing. My emotional needs seem to not matter; my sexual needs seemed to not matter.

I gave up on my dreams of meeting a good man. I was beyond questioning what was wrong with me. I accepted this is the way it was. Life was not fair, and good things happen to everyone but me. This was my story, and I stopped praying about it. My heart was frozen in that area. I suppose some would say this is a natural move of self-preservation. Others would suggest it would not necessarily be a bad thing to have barriers up; it would make you less vulnerable to be preyed on.

The issue with something I call 'HOPEbrokeness,' is that it can lead to apathy and ambivalence. I just did not care anymore. Which meant what the point of being a virgin was? If my future was electric gadgets and unattainable fantasies, why couldn't I run with wolves? I did not go out of my way to look for trouble, but you can trust trouble to find you.

HARRY

I met Harry randomly, and from the get-go, I knew he was not Christian. With some guys, you can just know from the walk. He was upfront and let me know very early on that he recognised we were from two different worlds. I tell you, there are times when non-believers are easier to deal with than Church brothers. They can be so straightforward. He explained that someone like me (educated, professional, ambitious) could not be interested in someone like him. He said he could add no value to my life (in his own words). But what he could do was have sex with me. I have never been propositioned before.

Yeah, I had been approached (by random strangers) on the road at a rate of one a year. Do understand that I had never been seriously propositioned before. I remember one day walking to my car with him. He was being his usual flirty self, and I was, quite frankly, flattered by the attention. Nothing just happens. I knew if I invited him to sit in my car and talk, I knew what would happen. But I found that in hopebrokeness, you simply do not care anymore. It feels like a sort of rebellious arrogance. Feels a lot like lust.

I could hear the Holy Spirit tell me not to do it, but I quenched Him.

> For Pentecostal church readers- Quenching Holy Spirit is not merely telling people to stop hollering in Church so we can make announcements. It is completely ignoring the Holy Spirit's instructions/ will when He speaks to you.

I kissed Harry that day. After a minute, he jumped out the car with this smug face like *that went as I expected*. I was in shock because the gap between my first two kisses was about 10 years.

Nothing much happened with Harry, sorry to have to bore you. It was a cat mouse situation; I wanted to see if being a "bad" girl would entice him into wanting a relationship with me. It did not. Over the next few months, we had a few stolen make-out sessions, no petting, or anything substantial. I remember kissing him good-bye one day, already knowing that I would not miss him. It was easy to phase him out because he was never in... in the first place.

We were from different universes. We both knew it and so did not invest much time and attention. It was like throwing a ball past a dog crying "fetch," the dog looking at you and the ball before going about his business. I think this was set up to divert me away from the path God had set me. I chose not to sleep with him, but there were times when I was tempted. Not the proudest season of my life.

MANNY

Now... this guy kind of descended on me like an eagle and scooped me up in his talons. This one was a bit different. Manny was a sweet dude, sensitive soul, intelligent, and very funny. We got on like a house on fire. He managed to pique my interest. His personality was so different; I think I lowered my defence.

Right from the start, in true Super Sara Sonic fashion, we ended up conversed intensely. You see, we had this chemistry, spark, and synergy evident to everyone who saw us together. There were these awkward moments when people would pick up our 'love' vibe. I remember a friend of his standing in-between us. Then randomly in the middle of small talk, he came out with, "are you two in love?" I think I was. I did not know what to make of the attention he was giving me. Give me a break, people he had potential.

We shared phone calls that lasted way past the call of platonic friendship, in my opinion. I am talking the most extended conversation was 8 hours. Eight hours! EIGHT HOURS????? What do you talk about for that long? Everything and nothing is the answer. I got on with my evening activities, cooking, and he went to the gym with me in his ear. We went out a lot. I felt it was refreshing to hang with someone who was not toxic.

Isn't it just like women to want to define everything very early on? I know there are some laid back women out there, but I am not one of them. So headstrong as ever; I confronted him about whether this was a friendship with future. I remember that night like it was yesterday. Yet again, I was telling another dude that I liked him. Sigh... facepalm. And basically, he denied any involvement in my crazy fantasies of something other than a platonic relationship. OUCHA!

At no point did I claim him or say he was the one. I just knew that I was attracted to him and appreciated our friendship. He knew how I felt but did not have a problem with it. There was a season of awkwardness as you would expect, but once the turbulence settled, the friendship recovered.

Friends were calling for me to stop talking to him altogether. Yet again I had my emotional claws out, and they were dug in real deep. I had just emerged from a very dark lonely season and did not want to be back there so soon. So I rationalised myself into staying in the friendship. I did not want to lose my new cheerleader and buddy. I decided that I would be a friend to him, and one day, perhaps he would review the situation and finally see me as a potential. I felt I could make it work.

I loved this guy to pieces, but we seriously fought like cats and dogs. I promise you every week he found a new way to hopscotch on my last nerve! God used him, I think to teach me a lot about myself. Our friendship did take a lot out of me. I was his "go-to" girl for advice, attention, affirmation, and encouragement. I felt needed, and that was enough... for a while.
He knew I liked him more than a friend. I was not strong enough to walk away, even though he had made it clear the feelings were not mutual. He basked in my attention like a Bichon Frise in a doggy salon bubble bath.

However, I soon buckled under the weight of a one-sided friendship. Manny told me that my expectations were too high. He could not and did not want to be there for me like I was for him.

This came to a head when I relocated abroad for work. I purposefully chose to sit back and wait to see if he would reach out to me, but he did not. We went from communicating every day before I left, to nothing for months. I was hurt, of course, and very angry.

I felt for all the time, prayer, and love I had deposited into the bank account of our friendship, I deserved more. I had attempted to make a withdrawal, and to my surprise, I was denied access. I do not feel anyone really knew how sad I was. It wounded me deeply to think that I was so dispensable.

(Years later, he did apologise for everything. But I did not wait for that apology to heal or forgive. I had to achieve closure by myself.)

DANNY

Danny was just a brief encounter. I was teetering on edge between self-pity and utter despair. I was trying to be positive by reading books, watching vlogs, and hanging out with the girls. I became obsessed with not caring about a single status because that is the exact moment your husband shows up. No matter how much I declared out loud that I did not want a man. I secretly wanted something good to happen to me.

Danny was not that something good to happen to me. Bless his heart, he was a good man, but we were not compatible. We ended up hanging out a few times. On one of those occasions, I do not believe he had any money. Sigh. He dared me to say something outlandish, threatening that he would not pay for the meal if I did not. Danny implied that he would 'dine and dash' if I did not play along. I was not sure how serious he was, so I decided to pay for him as well as myself. I received a stern rebuke from my sister. He was a man with some issues at the time. I went out with him because he was physically fit and thought I was attractive. We were not intellectually, socially, or spiritually compatible at all.

The main *ba dap dap* of the situation was that I was really turned on one day, and even though we both knew it was not going *there*, I wanted to experience a kiss again. (Yes I know I said the last time, was the last time) I dropped him home, and we were chilling in the car. He was talking, and I wanted a kiss.

(Guy is leant back slightly in the passenger seat, Girl is sat behind the wheel)

Guy: Sometimes I find it so hard to talk to God...
Girl: What is so hard about it?
Guy: Well, I just don't know what to say?

Girl: Tell Him about your day... He is not some ogre you know. He knows you so well. He has a major plan for your life.

(Girl edges closer to Guy)

Guy: That is deep you know, you think he actually has a plan for me?

Girl: Of course He does, you just need to ask him.

(Girl edges even closer to Guy)

Guy: What are you doing?

Girl: (Smirks) You know....

Guy: Yeah, I can read your body language but it is not happening.

Girl: Why?

Guy: Because what next? We are not going to be together.

Girl: Why not?

Guy: You know why!! ...besides I feel God's presence in this car.

Girl: What?

Guy: You are going to regret it. This is not what you want. What time is it? I have got to go.

Girl: Don't go!

(Guy starts to take off his seat belt.)

(CLICK)

Guy: What are you doing? (laughing)

Girl: Stay!

Guy: Do your parents know where you are? Lady, unlock the door.

(He fiddles with the door, it does not open)

You are not serious still. (He looks up to heaven and starts praying) Girl!

(Girl watches him play with mechanisms of the door. And he finally opens the door. She lunges and makes a grab for his arm)

Girl: Just one kiss

Guy: No! Your phone is ringing... it is your Dad. (Trying to shake Girl off) Girl, I got to go! Come on now!

(Girl releases his arm and Guy gets out. He stands in total amazement)

Guy: Ring me when you get home.

Girl: No! (Speeds off)

It could have been something like that. And if it was, I would like to clarify that what Girl did was 100% wrong. If that was the other way round, Girl could have claimed sexual harassment. I am grateful that Danny felt it was all hilarious. On a serious note, never put yourself or someone else in that position.

Whatever debate was going on about his spiritual maturity had to be put on the back burner because he stood up as an absolute man of God. He could have well and truly taken what was on offer and pushed me for more. He watched me drive off as if I was going to follow him to his house if he didn't. I was in the flesh, but I was not that far gone. Got home, and I felt so embarrassed. He was right, I would have regretted it.

He called me that night because I refused to text him to say I had got home safely. I made a point to sincerely apologise for my behaviour. He forgave me and then proceeded to make jokes. I took all the jokes, of course, because I put myself in that position.

Nothing became of Danny and me; he quickly became an acquaintance. We continued to talk as friends, but I was so embarrassed I did not really want to hang around him. He was a nice guy, and I thought I could support him from afar. I wish him all the best; he will make a woman very happy. He disclosed on one occasion that he knew that I was too spiritually mature for him, imagine even after the car stunt. I was far too accomplished, too educated, too whatever. I told him that he was a lion of a man with a good heart.

I have many more stories but that there are for another day. Your chronicles may be completely different. Your tales may be more extensive and dramatic than mine, but that is not the point. Thanks be to God that we are all saved by His grace. He has seen us through high and low times. We could have really been damaged messing about with the wrong one. But we came through and not return to folly! We are still standing and for that, I will ever be grateful to God.

REFLECTION

I have to reflect on events and cases all the time as a part of my job. It is a part of continued professional development. I hate it, but it is helpful for my growth as a physician. I think we should adopt the same protocol when looking at our lives. For those of you who keep a diary, you are amazing, and you are probably doing this already. If you Google the words "reflection model," it will bring up several psychologists designed models which detail a step by step exercise. Choose any one you like.

If you are like me, preferring the path of least resistance, aka easy way. The general principles of thinking about events in your life are:

➢ Contemplate what happened – Facts, be real
➢ How did it make you feel?
➢ What was good about the experience? What was bad?
➢ What did you learn? Good... Bad...

> ➢ What new things can you put in practice to improve your life experience?
> ➢ What else could you do to ensure that you are 'over' this event/person?

It is so simple but super practical for a woman who wants to break a harmful cycle. It does not work if you are not honest or do not take responsibility for your actions. I really do believe in counselling, because sometimes we are blind to our role in certain situations. We can become so fixated on certain parts of the story that we miss the bigger picture. I will repeat it... you cannot fix what you cannot see. Talking out loud to someone who you do not know, but trust can be so revealing. It does not necessarily have to be a Christian counsellor. Still, I prefer them because they value the spiritual aspect of life.

FORGIVENESS

When you go on a walk down memory lane, I guarantee it will dredge up emotions you did not even know existed. Reflection on previous events can cause you to relive any trauma you have not dealt with. It is amazing how resilient we are. We sometimes just suppress the pain and keep moving. But I believe during the reading of this book... God wants you to stop moving for a moment. It is time to see if unresolved issues are lurking in the shadows of your past.

There is no way I could have written this book if I had not forgiven or released from my heart every single one of those men I just mentioned. There are some I have not mentioned but them too. I used to wonder how you could forgive someone that you are not sure is even sorry? How can you be expected to get over something when you have no closure? Some of you have been through some heavy stuff and the person in question does not even logically deserve forgiveness!! I understand you.

The main thing is that forgiveness is not about the other person, it is really about you. It is about you being able to release negative emotions and thoughts for your own health.

Forgiveness is not just something God expects us to do because we are Christians. It is for your own benefit and freedom. You do not want to be tied to a massive dead thing. It adds to our emotional baggage, weighing us down in the journey of life. If simply thinking about the situation triggers pain and anger, that person still has power over you. That resentment and bitterness keep scars alive. You will not be able to heal correctly. That 'HOPEbrokeness' will sap the joy out of you, and that is no way to live.

'Forgiveness is not a feeling. It's a choice you consciously make. You have to decide to tell yourself, [they are] not worthy of one more ounce of my energy or thoughts. I am withdrawing my investment in bitterness and hatred to invest more fully in the people I love and care about. [They] may have had a hold on me, but now I am choosing to shake [them] loose. I am taking back the ability to decide who I am, what I think, how I feel, and whom I focus on. That's where my power comes from. I will not let anyone else turn my heart cold or change who I am.' - Dr. Phil McGraw (1)

> [Mat 6:15 NIV]
> But if you do not forgive others their sins,
> your Father will not forgive your sins.

How can we expect God to forgive us when we refuse to forgive our trespassers? God will judge unforgiveness as unconfessed sin. Forgiving them does not change whatever they did that was wrong. But it will change your life for the better, releasing peace and taking back control. You are making your heart fully available to the real man coming along.

I do not know about you, but sometimes I say things I do not mean. I pray things that I do not act out, and that is a problem. Never forget that God looks beyond the words and looks into the thoughts and intents of the heart. In plain English, you cannot fool him into believing something that is not true. If you are not over a guy, just say it, so the Holy Spirit can help through it.

MOVING ON

Once you have made your peace, move on. All the way on. My sister and I got into a discussion about keeping old pictures. She is a 'wipe everything off your phone' girl. I realised that I struggled to do the same. I used to like having old pictures. It was a part of my life. I do not remember a lot of details from my childhood for some reason, but having little mementos means I can appreciate where I have come from. She did not think it was healthy and may be offensive to the future man in my life.

Can I be honest? Or even more accurate? I have not had that much action in the romance department, as you know. I felt that having old pictures made me feel like I had a social life. However, I could see where sis was coming from. As I look back at the pictures, what am I thinking? Am I reminiscing? Am I torturing myself with should have, would have or could have thoughts? Do the photos bring back memories of embarrassing events? How does looking at this picture really make me feel? To be honest, most of those responses and emotions were not encouraging.

Once you have made a note of the lessons learnt. It is time to clean house. A clean house makes room for new memories to be stored.

I did not want to miss out on a better life because my mind was stuck in the past. So you know what? I decided to delete delete delete! Any picture that I belonged to a guy I had romantic feelings for was erased. I felt I was giving up evidence or memory of someone who once brought me joy. But it brought me to greater faith, I believed the best was yet to come.

The thing about pictures is that it is just a freeze-frame of one moment. If we are not careful, we will pretend that this person was the right one for us. We overlook or purposefully ignore the pain they put us through. When our emotional buttons get pressed it could lead to us to comfort ourselves with our past. Out of loneliness, we may just call that ex. We may think about the sexual stuff we did with that person. Thoughts can be so powerful. So guess what? The smartest thing is to remove that trigger. Take authority over your thoughts and help yourself out by removing reminders of the past.

Although your heart may have been mishandled, if you have recovered, declare that chapter in your life is over. There are no returns to the past and no double backs. Do not stay in communication with someone that is not good for you, hoping they will transform. *If he ain't wearing a nappy, baby, you can't change him*. Woman of destiny, when God cuts you loose, stay loose. There is no way you can heal from being 'HOPEbroken' if you find yourself stuck in a time warp. You cannot even see the good guys because you are preoccupied with the imprint of a bad one.

Now I think about it; it is a bit like Lot's wife looking back at Sodom and Gomorrah. She was lovingly rescued from a place of evil and corruption doomed for destruction. God was offering her a new life. She was literally on her way out, but then she disobeyed by looking back with regret. Lot's wife felt that what was behind her was better than what was to come. Sadly, she was judged by God, who turned her into a pillar of salt. She did not make it to that better future. Learn from her; that is why this story is in the Bible. Run to your future, which is much better than what you are leaving behind.

Build a monument

In the Old Testament, the saints of old built monuments to commemorate something God said or did. Abraham built one when God gave Him the promise that he would become the father of many nations. Joshua had the people of Israel create one when they crossed over the River Jordan. Why? It was an act of worship to God; it served as a reminder to be thankful for what God has done. It showed the enemy that their God had come through for them. I can imagine that in the low times when their faith dipped, they looked at that structure, which reminded them of God's power and consistency. I love that principle, and I intentionally do the same.

Some of you may keep diaries and journals (I still to this day do not know the difference between a diary and a journal), but it is a brilliant practice. This book, for me, is a monument. In the movie War Room, the prayer warrior Clara Williams had a frame proudly displayed in her home, and she wrote in it whenever God answered her prayer.

Go on a holiday, do a photoshoot, something fun, make it meaningful. So when you look back on it, it inspires gratitude. It is essential to do something to celebrate the fact that you are still alive and breathing. You may have gone through hell and high water. But when you woke this morning, it was a brand NEW day. Where there is life, there is the hope of a better tomorrow. Get into the routine of giving God thanks even if all the ducks are still not lining up.

"Your destiny is never tied to anyone that left you. Let them go." One of my favourite TD Jakes quotes. Do I have regrets? YES. Big time. Some say there is no such thing as mistakes. Yes, there are. There are some things I just got wrong and suffered as a consequence. If I had a choice, I would not do it again. It was not fun, but I made it. You will make it too.

No matter what shipwreck is in your past, you got to stride towards the future. Each day is a new opportunity to change your present and dictate what your tomorrow will be. In your future, as far as it is in your control, you will not allow men to manhandle you. You are to be treated like a Queen because that is who you are. You know your worth! You have learned from past mistakes. Now you set the standard of love according to what you know you deserve.

Chapter Two

_____HOPEbroken_____

Heartbreak, in itself, is recognised as a medical condition. Science helps us to understand that the brain perceives rejection as physical pain. Stress can cause high cortisol levels, disturb sleep patterns, and even lower our immune systems. Yes! I am saying it can physically weaken you to the point where you also struggle to fight off a cold, let alone the challenges you face in everyday life. (2)

I have seen and managed people with a heart condition called Takutsubo Syndrome. Due to emotional distress, they have a kind of heart attack where the bottom part of their heart balloons. There is legitimate chest pain leading them to present like a typical heart attack (the one where heart muscles die from lack of oxygen). We put them on an intense treatment pathway, medications, scans, and a visit to the CATH lab. An angiogram is an investigation where dye is injected into the bloodstream. Doctors watch the blood go through the different blood vessels supplying the heart using a sort of x-ray machine. In Takutsubo syndrome, there is usually no blood vessel blockage (which typically causes a heart attack.) We only find out it is not a typical life-threatening heart attack at this stage. The patients with Takustubo syndrome do not need further treatment; they will recover in their own time. Wow!

I felt I had to make up a term to describe the emotional state I felt each time a situation-ship (not an official relationship) blew up in my face. I needed to mark the season when your spirit is broken as well as your heart. This pain drills down into that eternal part of you that seats your soul, will, and mind. Many situations can break your heart, but this is the term I coined to describe the spiritual low caused by a romantic disaster. Those failed expectations of a relationship go beyond HEARTbreak to HOPEbrokeness.

> Proverbs 18:14
> The human spirit can endure a sick body but who can bear a crushed spirit?

The first thing to note is that HOPEbrokeness starts as being compartmentalised. I would find that I was satisfied with my career and optimistic about my family. But when it came to matters of the heart, I was a wreck. My cynical perspective was strictly reserved for my love life. I had lost faith that things in my social life were ever going to get better for me. That romantic hopeful innocent girl had been beaten down to nothing.

I recognise that there are many reasons one could experience being HOPEbroken. Job lamented that 'a man's days are short and full of trouble.' Traumatic things happen to everyone. No one is minimising the grief that comes with losing a loved one or battling through an illness. Those things can bring unimaginable pain.

God tells us that in all things, we must give thanks. I guarantee you someone has it worst. But at the same time, YOUR specific life narrative gives you YOUR life experience. If something makes you sad... It makes YOU sad. You have to build up your resilience to hardship and disappointments based on YOUR experience. I wanted to focus on one area of my life that has been a consistent dark desert. I realise that there is more to life than relationships, but this was one of MY battlegrounds.

I reckon that there is a stage beyond reactive sadness or disappointment that is hard to come back from. It is when you stop crying, but that aspiration, joy, optimism is permanently muted. Deep down, because you are depressed, you develop an ambivalent attitude to life. You are not necessarily overtly bitter, but you have accepted things the way they are and have no desire to change it. It is the apathetic state where you believe all things are possible, but not for you.

For me, HOPEbrokeness encapsulates an entire range of negative emotions. Being rejected by various guys took the joy out of me like a kid laying into a piñata. I knew I had low self-esteem, to begin with, but my heart and sense of worth took another hit each time I was rejected. The way I saw myself was influenced by how others treated me.

I was that foolish man Jesus spoke about who built his house on sandy land. When the storms of life came to my house... my heart... fell flat. The foundation of my self-esteem was built on what men thought of me, which is not healthy. There is no way I could be a mighty woman of God, yet so vulnerable and weak in my social life. God showed me the extent of my vulnerability, and this had to be addressed.

Apathetic	Angry	Jealousy	Self pity	Anxiety
Lonely	Labile	Rebellious	Desperate	Worthless
Bored	Hopeless	Risk Taking behaviour	Fearful	Rejected

Fig 1: [A table to highlight the typical emotions one experiences when they are HOPEbroken.]

If you consistently experience these emotions daily, sit up, and take notice. Something is wrong, and things do not have to remain that way. When you feel your social life is not exciting or enjoyable, you may do something reckless to spice it up. Anything to take a breather or distract you from the pain or disappointment you think you cannot overcome. I felt like it was an emotional state of numbness. In low times I did not care about holding on to my self-respect and morals. This is not the best way to navigate through singlehood.

"You don't make friends with salad!!" LOL There is nothing wrong with salad. This is just a long standing Simpsons joke in my family. It means it is harder to attract positive people when you are not at your best. (Again, there is nothing wrong with salad. I live on the stuff!) Living in a state of HOPEbrokeness is not conducive to making the most appropriate decisions with your heart. You can indeed overcome my friend but you need to confront the real issues.

It is time to confront the four horsemen of the HOPEbroken Apocalypse.

HOPEbroken: Jealous

I never considered myself the jealous type. Jealousy or envy says to God; You should not have done that for them. I think Joyce Meyer put it that way, and it has always stuck with me. I am the generation that unfortunately witnessed the birth of reality TV. Reality TV is a step beyond music videos. Hollywood tried (and continues to work) to convince you that gorgeous, physically perfect women, live exciting, fulfilled, dramatic lives. It was supposed to be "real" so I felt that if I emulated some of their looks and behaviours, I too would have an exciting fulfilled dramatic life. I am sure I am not the only young woman who attempted to live vicariously through them.

I was the jealous type, though, sitting there overweight with stretch marks all over me. Wide feet, wide-nosed, black knees, eczema, dark-skinned. I felt I had no chance of attracting a man. Watching these models and rapper/athlete WAGS (Wife and girlfriends) on a TV screen was one thing; it was another thing seeing pretty women in real life. Why did God have to make her so beautiful?? Why are her teeth perfect and mine crooked? How come she eats like an elephant and is the size of a gazelle? I was very self-conscious in public and never felt good enough no matter what I put on. Some people stand naked before the mirror and criticise themselves. I did not even need to get naked, that would be a waste of time; I looked a disaster in clothes; there was no point stripping down.

I think back to myself, staring into my younger sisters' wardrobe. She had an outfit I wanted, but my poor mum (not financially lol) could not find it in my size. Oh yes, some shiny pink satin trousers. It was paired with a velvet black vest top and matching shrug with some diamanté detail. Why was I staring at it? I was considered much trouble I would get into if I took a pair of scissors and cut it up! Good sense and fear of my mother held me back that day. I remember closing the door slowly and quietly. I was 12 at the time; she was 6. HEY! The outfit was dope, in the 00's shiny and velvety stuff were very much in fashion.

This is what jealousy does:
- It compares itself to others
- It obsesses and focuses on things outside of your control
- It creates dissatisfaction and resentment that can push you to do destructive things to make yourself feel better
- Ten times out of ten, if you do those cruel things, you feel worse.

- ➤ It prevents you from being happy for other people
- ➤ You soon devote your energy to disliking, even hating people.
- ➤ It blocks your blessings
- ➤ Its stench pushes people away from you
- ➤ It will consume you.

James 3:16

For where you have envy and selfish ambition, there you find disorder and every evil practice.

ADVICE: Do not allow the seeds of jealousy to grow.

I stand by this belief tall and firm: "No one can take what God has promised me." I am going to need you to repeat that. Clear your throat and speak it out loud. "NO ONE CAN TAKE FROM ME WHAT GOD HAS PROMISED ME." When we make declarations, we have to believe. Our declarations have power because it is based on God's word. God has promised to perfect that which concerns you. So here goes the scripture.

> Jeremiah 29:11
> For I know the plans that I have for you,
> plans that are good and not evil, to give you an
> expected end.

I tend to have a very skeptical response when people say *Miss Thing stole my man from me.* Honey, if your boyfriend went to her, he was never yours in the first place. The best thing you could do is let her keep him. God has an upgrade coming for you. To be clear, I am not talking about marriage. Adultery is entirely another subject.

No one can take what God has promised you. I do not understand why women turn into UFC fighters over a man? For example (now this is going to sound harsh, just know I still love you.) even if he is your child's father, there is nothing you can do to make him stay.

Another baby will not do it. There comes a time you have to let him go if he wants out. I can only imagine what you have invested, but you deserve a man that wants to be with you. Keep your self-respect by refusing to clash with another woman if you consider sharing a man with another woman. There is a strong possibility you may be HOPEbroken.

A hopeful woman does not compete. She recognises she is the prize to be won. She will not ferociously attack another woman for a man's attention. I appreciate the genuine emotional trauma of being abandoned in motherhood, but this behaviour will not do as a woman. HOPEbrokeness can manifest as anger, jealousy, and competitive behaviour.

I reiterate you do not need to be jealous of anyone. You do not need to compete against anyone for your victory. If that sister won, you could win too. If that brother is getting his own house, it does not stop you from buying yours. There is enough success in this world to go around. God, who gives every good gift, can surely supply all your needs. I just want to reassure you that what is yours is yours, and the only one who can forfeit blessings.... is you. God intends for you to receive all the Abrahamic blessings. You are His kid, and He will take care of you.

Some of us are jealous, and we do not even realise it. The Holy Spirit may need to bring it to your attention, so please listen to Him. Jealousy will stop you from being blessed. Uproot every emotional weed relating to resentment. Do not entertain selfish thoughts. Intentionally practice complimenting others. Applaud another women's looks and hairstyles. Focus on nurturing the grass on your side of the fence instead of watching other people's lawn grow.

You have to be so intentional about kicking jealousy out your life because she is a sneaky one. Learn to say positive things when your Facebook friends' milestones and achievements appear in your newsfeed. You will have your news to share soon enough, but in the meanwhile, practice celebrating other people.

> Never become tired of saying... I am happy for you. AND BE HAPPY FOR THEM! Your breakthrough is around the corner. Do not allow bitterness or fatigue to delay your testimony.

HOPEbroken: Low Self Esteem

Low self-esteem is something I was not born with but developed in early childhood. I am sure my parents did their utmost best because they still do spoil me... and I am a grown woman. I do not doubt the pureness and consistency of their love. So this low self-esteem was not triggered by anything that went on inside my home. I know someone reading may have grown up in a hostile environment. But for me, it was leaving the cradle of safety and venturing out into school. Peers ostracised me. I was taller than them, fat and smart. I used to do my homework at lunchtime rather than go out to play. There were good days, but my self-esteem was very low. I did not think I was good enough, mainly because of my appearance. I blamed the fat because it was something everyone could see. My weight may have had no bearing on how I was treated in reality, but as a child, that is how I looked at the whole thing; and it negatively affected me.

My parents tried everything they could. Counselling, making up Princess day, holidays, toys. There was nothing I physically needed, but I hated myself. And get this, because I hated myself, I ate. Then as I put on weight, I hated myself. I sit here typing this still overweight. I am in the middle of my FIFTH weight loss attempt and not going to sugar coat, it is horrible carrying a weakness everyone can see.

I used to study psychology, which told me about the fight between nature and nurture. Personality and personal experiences. Internal and external factors. Twins could grow up in the same environment, but one will turn out this way and another due to personality differences. Alternatively, it could be that their personal experiences within the same environment differ. Some people are just more resilient and have good self-esteem despite challenging life obstacles. Other people, like myself, did not handle rejection and complex social situations well.

If you do not have healthy self-esteem, you are not motivated to protect yourself. You want to feel better, so you look for fulfilment anywhere and everywhere. For me, it was food and getting attention from men. For someone else, it can be clubbing, alcohol, sex, stealing, drugs. There is an idea of escapism from reality, even though the experience is transient and expensive. You find yourself looking for an emotional high. These activities are merely distractions that are not sustainable. They give you a moment of euphoria, but will not hold your focus or happiness. You will have to move on to the next thing, and the next thing, your overall enjoyment of life can diminish.

Low self-esteem craves attention like oxygen and does not discriminate against who provides it. Guys can sense a woman with low self-esteem a mile away. And they will use this knowledge to their advantage to get what they want. And often it is sex. A woman with low self-esteem is more likely to sleep with them. They just want to feel wanted, and guys may not have to work hard to get them into bed. And when they have got what they wanted, many will not hesitate to leave without looking back.

These shallow men can quickly pick up if the woman is needy, clingy, weak, lacking in personal drive and determination. Low self-esteem will cause a woman to hang unto the relationship like a dog with a bone; because it makes them feel good about themselves. They give up all their power to their men, and when the men leave, their reason for existing leaves as well. That is not who God says you are, and that is not how He wants you to be treated by men.

If you allow men to define who you are to validate your worth, you risk losing your identity if they change their mind. Man did not create you, so they can struggle to see your actual value. They may have difficulty in understanding who you are or what your purpose is in life. They have no right to tell what you deserve. Your self-esteem is NOT supposed to be based on people's opinions of you.

Low Self Esteem:
- Is a failure to understand or accept what God says about you
- Implies that you do not value who you are
- Causes you to not take care of yourself properly
- Craves attention for someone or something to boost it

ADVICE: Self Esteem can be restored to a healthy level.

Your self-esteem should be healthy because of what God says about you. Psalms 132 says God fearfully and wonderfully made you. I will be honest; I knew about that scripture but did not accept it as personal truth. My faith in God and my confidence in God had to grow. I always wondered about people born with defects and illnesses, because it almost seems as if God dropped the ball with them. Wrong, even with your imperfections and flaws, you are still wonderfully made and a great purpose.

I do not have an explanation for children born with life-threatening illnesses. It would seem it is apart of the fall out of living in a sinful world. I do not know why God allows it, but He is sovereign. If I could understand everything about Him and His ways, He would not be God. But when I consider the number of babies who make it into the world, it is nothing short of a miracle. You are not here today by accident. God thought about making you before the foundations of the world were laid, and He designed your life. There is nothing you face that you cannot overcome. You are so precious that God sent His own begotten Son to redeem you. You are special and unique as your fingerprint. There is no one better than you, and you are not better than anyone else.

God may have to take you on a journey to discover these truths, but when you do, you build your self-esteem upon the Solid Rock. When storms during dating/relationships come, your love for yourself and the belief that you are worthy of good things will remain.

Having healthy self-esteem protects you against lowering your standards. It is one of the ways you guard your heart. You know what you deserve and will not settle far from your expectation. This woman will avoid entertaining foolishness. She will not return to a past failed relationship because she knows she can do better. She would rather wait for better than to expose herself to more misery. A confident woman loves her own company and does not need to be rescued from her life of singleness.

It was only after I fell in love with myself, warts, and all that I could begin my weight loss seriously. I felt I was worthy of taking care of me even if no man 'wanted' me. I was not going to abuse myself any longer. I have one life, and I did not want to waste it being miserable. If I could not love myself, how could I expect someone to love me and to love me, right? I needed to set the standard on how I should be treated. So I made I concerted effort to take care of myself, body, mind, and soul. What about you?

Love is the first fruit mentioned in the Galatians 5:25. The reason why it was mentioned first is that all the other fruit/characteristics of Christian stem from this root. If you are having trouble loving yourself, ask God to show you who you are. When He does, believe Him. This is the foundation of your identity.

The Devil is also called the accuser of the brethren. He spends his time cussing you out and bringing up your past. He tells you that you are not lovable or significant to God because you may find yourself in challenging circumstances. But allow me to reinforce that your current conditions do not determine God's love for you. His passion for you is unconditional, sacrificial, pure, potent, profound, healing, and liberating. You do not have to earn His love, as Jesus died for you while you were a sinner. It is not based on your performance or your achievements. It is not based on your looks or your gifts.

There is nothing you can do to make God love you any more or any less than He already does. You belong to Jesus, and He is coming back for you one day. No matter who rejected you, Christ accepts you just for who you are. He said, come as you are to Him, with all your baggage and sinful flaws. His arms are always open to you, and you will still be His beautiful daughter. If God can love you, you can love you. Make sure you do.

HOPEbroken: Bitter

Have you ever tasted a Jamaican drink called Bitters? My Dad loves it and used to drink it for its supposed health benefits. I hated that rancid concoction that he would dare us to swig for money. Oh yes and Cerasse tea, my parents used to get the real bush and boil it. It stunk up the whole house and made me gag every fresh brew.

Tasting something bitter has that shock value; it invades your taste buds, and you instantly regret your decision. You spit and spit, or you might try other foods/drinks to mask the taste. Repulsive and offensive. You are keen to avoid a repeat of that experience too soon. When you do not recover from past negative experiences and refuse to forgive, it creates an invisible spiritual stench. When folks interact with you, it may leave a bitter taste in their mouth.

> Unforgiveness breeds bitterness and we have all met a bitter woman right? Unpleasant.

Bitterness:
- ➢ Often expresses itself through unprovoked anger
- ➢ Cannot coexist with joy

- Is an unpleasant personality that will ultimately push people away
- Creates a negative perception of the present
- Can breed a pessimistic attitude
- Can cause negative speech
- Can cause you to lose sight of your dreams

ADVICE: It will hurt letting go of whatever made you bitter in the first place, but that pain will fade.

You cannot enjoy life to its fullest when you are weighed down by unresolved issues. That emotional baggage will happily break your back. Every day you ignore that hostility and sourness; you allow yourself to be held back from the abundant life Christ wants you to experience.

The process of getting rid of bitterness starts in prayer. You have to ask God to do a deep cleanse of your heart. It begins with a sound decision to let something that angers or has hurt you go. David penned these words about another situation in his life, but I love the

77

request he made of God. 'Create in me a clean heart and renew a right spirit within me.' God will do it, just like that:: finger snap:: Thanos style.... Maybe not the best example, but you get the idea.

There must be a renewal of your thinking and an intentional effort to love where there was hate. No more fighting. No more hostility. No more bad-mindedness. Give up that secret desire to see the people that caused your pain to get their comeuppance. Vengeance is in the hand of the Lord, for He is a righteous judge.

That unfair situation you found yourself in does not have power over you. Leave it at all at the foot of the cross where Christ has given you dominion over all things. Holy Spirit also has another name called the "Comforter." He is right there to fill your life with a peace that will surpass your understanding. Holding on to negative emotions keeps the emotional scars alive. Pull out the thorn, and this will activate healing from the inside out.

If you surrender to God's will with your whole heart, He will make sure you get what He has promised you. God can and will restore everything you lost. You are not a victim; you are a victorious woman of God. Shut up, Devil!!! There is so much more to look forward to because life will get better.

Take back your joy in Jesus' name!

Praise and worship helped me heal. The more I sang and spent time giving God thanks for what I did have, the more bitterness faded away. One moment with the King can change your life. His remarkable presence makes you feel better; you can go to Him morning, noon, or night. In your bedroom or on the train traveling to work. It is enjoyable to love God through worship. It connects you to His Presence and brings freedom.

HOPEbroken: Frustration

Frustration is the archenemy of joy. Its job is to kill, steal, and destroy your peace. It can grow like a weed in the cracks of your life. Wherever there is a perceived injustice in your life, perhaps something that you feel you have little control over, it is a natural response to react negatively. But if you do not get a handle on that disequilibrium, it will evolve into bitterness. You already know all about bitterness.

For me, I resented the fact that it appeared that I did not have a choice in being single. I felt I had like zero options and an opportunity to be in a relationship. I never had a friend that liked me back or a decent, respectful guy who wanted to take me out to eat. I suspect that God wanted it this way because he knew I would take the first offer. He knew I would settle.

I was the girl who had grown up with guys high fiving her as a girl pal or saying she was too 'churchy churchy.' If you had been overwhelmed by rejection throughout your whole life, it might have been enough to make you think that you were unlikeable. You perhaps would understand my wish to come up for air at the first opportunity.

I felt God was restricting my opportunities for a relationship. I remember Him running guys away for me. I threw myself like a torpedo at some dudes, and they suddenly had a change of heart. They did not even want to touch me at all. It was as if there was an invisible shield to the naked eye that repelled them.

I thank God because He has been faithful to save me and protect my destiny. But it was frustrating. Interestingly, I was re-baptised in 2015 at 26 years old because I felt I wanted to turn over a new leaf. I remember saying in my testimony before the dipping, that as the Apostle Paul, I was a prisoner of the Lord Jesus Christ. I will be honest in admitting that there are some days of 'incarceration,' that I feel like I do not want to be here.

I can become depressed when I allow frustration to grow and take over my heart. It is a natural and sometimes appropriate response to a situation, but it has to be transient. A feeling that just passes through because you refuse to entertain it. It cannot cohabitate with faith and peace.

I have previously suffered from road rage finding myself in some situations where drivers have come out of their car and banged on my front screen/window.... Twice. I have made stupid, dangerous decisions on the road based on the fact I did not want to wait. Not to over spiritualise, you know I do not like doing that. But God revealed to me that there was an undercurrent of tension in my life because I was not at peace with His character development methods.

I perceived that I had no control over the situation. I felt I was being battered to and fro, which hurt me. So whenever I found myself in trivial scenarios where I did not have control, it invoked an overreaction. My attitude says: 'I refuse to keep sitting here having this happen to me, so I am going to do something.' My patience was the size of a chicken nugget.

I realised that it was not acceptable for me to keep living like this. I am a benefactor of the grace God, so that frustrated, impatient attitude had to go.

If frustration has its way, it will cause you to react irrationally to everyday life situations, and this can cause consequences you do not want. You are unable to demonstrate God's faithfulness and gentle character in your life. How will people know you are a real Christian? How can we quote scriptures one day and be swearing at people the next?

That lack of consistency may turn people off the idea of Christ. They may fear that they will wind up miserable like you. We cannot be calling ourselves women of purpose and power but walk around two seconds away from complete combustion. The Bible says anger rests in the bosom of a fool. I did not want to be considered a fool, so frustration had to go.

How to beat the four horsemen of the

HOPEbroken Apocalypse

PATIENCE

Patience is underrated because it is interpreted as inactivity. That is inaccurate; the amount of self-control that is required to wait on God is immense. It requires mental strength, obedience, and trust to hold your position. It is like a duck in the water; from the top, the duck appears still, but under the water, his little legs are going like Usain Bolt. It is an action that allows God to take action on your behalf.

Patience is essential if you want a breakthrough in your life. The Devil cannot tempt or distract a patient believer. He cannot set out traps for you or bait because you will not bite. You refuse to settle for anything less than God's best or stray from the path He has set for you because you trust His heart more than your current circumstances and past.

Patience will cause you to make the right decision at the right time. You will not miss opportunities. Do not rush life. We should not rush one of the most important decisions of life. Delayed gratification is something that children find it hard to understand. They want their treat, and they want it now, even if it means missing out on something better later. But as mature women in the faith, we must put the childish things away. Why accept a Mcdonald's meal because you are hungry; when you know you have a delicious, nutritious meal waiting for you at home? The rushed choice will only satisfy for a short while and carries consequences you may not want to pay. Trust God that everything He promised you... will come to you at the right time.

Being patient does not imply that you are weak, but it means you are strong. Strong enough to stand when everything around is saying fall. Patience is a core spiritual muscle. It keeps you going amid your trials and tests. If you have no core strength at the gym, you are limited in how much cardio you can do. Your muscles will fatigue before you can accomplish your goals. God is saying run your race with endurance.

Paul encourages us not to grow weary in doing good because if we faint not... we will receive our reward. Consistency and repetition is the hallmark of champion athletes during training. Take it day by day, and recognise that God is getting the glory every step you take in life.

Patience is a mental discipline. It is a psychological safeguard that the Holy Spirit has to help you activate. It is a segment of fruit of the Holy Spirit. A commentator made a point that there are not nine different fruits of the holy spirit, it is one fruit with nine different parts. And that really all of them grow at the same time. I dare to disagree because I think the different segments grow at different rates. Sometimes I am kind, but I am not able to suffer long.

I digress; the Holy Spirit is responsible for your maturation, for you cannot grow on your own. Do you remember your emotional first prayer of repentance where you accepted Jesus as your saviour? You started a journey, and it will not stop till death, physical or spiritual.

Spiritual death separation from God. It is a decision to turn back from serving Him. To live a life of disobedience and rebellion to His commands.

The Holy Spirit will guide you through the daily process of growth. You have to be humble and teachable. He will not change you against your will; it is an equal partnership on both sides. I made an intentional decision to study and apply the word of God to my life. If I was going to beat road rage, I had to practice responding to circumstances like someone who has the mind of Christ. You have to look at the situation from a different point to control your thought life appropriately.

Life can be unpredictable and complicated; you have to deal with the unexpected. Life happens. It rains on the just and the unjust. You can easily be caught in a less than ideal situation. So what next? Well, patience perfected, intercepts your thoughts like a defender on a basketball court. You cannot control what happens at times, but you can adapt your response to it. It improves your coping skills.

For example, it is raining outside, and you do not have an umbrella. Rain to me without hair protection is a disaster. I could throw a tantrum when my hair gets wet, and this can put me in a bad mood all day. Or I could roll my eyes at the fact I have no umbrella and then refuse to get mad and stressed out. It is a filter for the negativity.

Patience is based on God's word. It is based on *believing* God's word to be exact. If you think that all things work together for your good, then you understand that your current battles will not last. You simply have to WAIT for the good to manifest. If you believe that God plans to prosper you if you are currently feeling harmed, then it is not the end of your story, your prospering has to come. That belief in His word, we call it faith, OVERRIDES the reality that you are experiencing.

Patience is the Godly response to situations that tests your faith. To everything, there is a time and season. You may be in a very testing trial, but it is time-sensitive. There will come a time when it HAS to change for God's word to be the truth. Therefore patience is a resilient, positive attitude that refuses to relinquish joy when challenged by adverse situations. It comes from having faith in God's word. It has the power to remain faithful TO God when under emotional fatigue. It is a discipline. It is something that can be learnt. When you have mastered it through the Holy Spirit's work, it allows you to stabilise your emotional response to life.

When you are patient:

➤ You allow joy to do its work.

➤ It will protect your heart against pretenders/ double agents.

➤ You enjoy life more

➤ It will reduce stress

➤ It will help you evaluate things objectively

➤ You will make better decisions

➤ You are not easily fooled

➤ You are not desperate

ADVICE: Frustration should be transient with patience as your usual attitude. It is human to REACT frustrated, but your RESPONSE is to be patient. You can control your response.

JOY

Did you see the film "Inside Out?' It was a fantastic children's film. I think I enjoyed it more than my God-daughter. I remember her asking me, "Auntie, why are you crying?" Joy was depicted by a happy-go-lucky girl/alien thing who lives inside the human head. She is responsible for making her human, a little girl called Sophie happy. She was in charge of all the other emotions: anger, sadness, disgust, fear. She had her work cut out for her because it was her job to make the best of every situation, no matter what was thrown at Sophie. I promise it will bless you do watch it if you have not seen it yet.

Joy is a positive, life giving, hopeful, smiling attitude based on the fulfilment of God's Word in your life. It is consistent satisfaction and contentment, which means that it does not disappear with evolving circumstances. People cannot give you joy, and conversely, they cannot take it away. Once you have joy, it is up to you not to give it up.

Joy is consistent. Happiness is based on circumstances. Happiness comes and goes; you can spend your whole life pursuing happiness but never capture it. Even if you get everything you have ever wanted, you may still feel unhappy. It fades because that emotional high starts to reduce as you get used to your new circumstances. Or it may be that a tragedy/drama/upset strikes and topples the balance. Joy is an anchor; it does not move. It is a part of your foundation. You can lose everything but not lose your satisfaction, and so maintain your praise for God and His marvellous plan for your life.

Joy:

- Makes it possible to enjoy being single
- Will keep you from being depressed
- Will protect you from looking to the world for contentment
- Will fuel you as you pass through difficult seasons in your life
- Allows you to laugh when you don't have everything you want
- Prevents you from being jealous over peoples lives
- Will enable you to feel satisfied in life.

ADVICE: Joy can be triggered by playing the 'grateful' game. Name fifty things that are going right in your life. From being able to smell, detect colours with your eyes, roof over your head, an indoor toilet, clean air to breathe, etc. Gratitude lifts your attitude!

PEACE

Peace is not the absence of chaos. Peace is calm amid the disorder. Everything does not have to have be peaceful for YOU to be full of peace. Christ says if you keep your mind on Him, He will keep you in perfect soul harmony. He will sustain you in a position of comfort despite your environment.

I think about Peter walking out to Jesus on the waves, what a brave guy, that guy had big-time faith! But the moment he took his eyes off Jesus, he began to sink. The moment we push God to the side and fixate on our problems. The moment we fill our lives with activities and leave no time for intimacy with God... we drown. Plain and simple. It is hard to have peace when you are disconnected from the Prince of peace, the peace giver, Jesus Christ.

Peace is the assurance that God is control. Relax, God is in control! Relax! It is impossible to have stress and peace at the same time. Sometimes it comes when we give up the driving seat of our lives. I found it difficult as a control freak to allow God to take full control of my life. The pressure of making sure everything turns out ok was too much to bear. I had to let Jesus take the wheel so I could hold on to peace.

Peace allows you to rest. Jesus said come unto me all ye who are weary and heavy laden, and I will give you rest. The disciples, as I would be, were shocked to find Jesus asleep on a boat during a life-threatening storm. Jesus knew who He was and what power He had. Do you know who Jesus is? Do you remember that He has all authority? Never forget that He is on your boat, so guess what? You can sleep. You can sleep when you do not know how your bills are going to be paid. You can sleep when no arms are holding you in the middle of the night. You can sleep when there is craziness happening at your job.

My dear sisters, you do not have to be in control to have peace; you just got to have faith in the one whose Hands, hold the whole world. Nothing escapes His attention and He has invested so much in you. You can one hundred percent rely on God to be present. He is omnipresent and all knowing.

Peace:

- ➢ Stress dissolver
- ➢ Allows you to sleep
- ➢ Settles your heart when it has been disappointed
- ➢ Peace allows your hope to heal
- ➢ Leaves no room for anger
- ➢ Helps you surrender your life to God
- ➢ Stops you fighting your own battles on your own

ADVICE: Write down the things that actively cause you to feel anxious. Use them as your basis for prayer for 21 days. Present them to the Lord and actively cast your cares on Him. Study your bible. Holy Spirit will lead you to the relevant promises to relieve your doubt. God is capable of meeting your needs.

I intentionally did not explore mental illness. However mental health is a very important topic. If you feel that you are not coping very well or if your feel suicidal, please do not suffer in silence. Be encouraged that it can get better. Do not give up!

Please do speak to a friend, counsellor, Church leader as well as your local GP (medical doctor) for further support and management.

Jesus is the ultimate healer, but there is no shame in taking medication if you deem it to be appropriate. I was offered antidepressants a few years ago, and I had to make a decision. Just because you start medication for a condition does not mean that you have to stay on it forever. I have seen lots of patients successfully weaned off their medication under the surveillance of their doctor.

> When Jesus healed the leper He said show yourself to the priest, this was for verification. So yes even when God has healed you get that written report from the doctor as a testimony! Jesus still heals! Never lose hope!

God can heal people who take medication. I do not understand how some people can discourage others from taking medication that God gave man creative power to develop. We quickly pray for people who have diabetes on medication, hoping that God will heal them. There should be no stigma attached to someone who is depressed and on medication. God can heal them, and they can taper off their regime, wholly delivered.

Victory is Yours

Hopebrokeness is a real thing. The right set of circumstances can cause it to happen to any of us. When it rains, sometimes it can pour. The downpour can be so torrential it almost washes you away. You lose your confidence that you will ever be truly happy again. Those four HOPEbroken horsemen can ride through, right after a personal crisis, and you may question the point of trying. God cares about you and will not leave you in that oppressive state. The Holy Spirit has the power to defeat those four horsemen, and you can get up again.

In the low times, realise that even though God is still working on you, you are still a masterpiece. Flaws and all. Woman of God, you are loved and worthy of love. Daughter of Zion, you are whole, validated, and fully capable of getting back on your feet.

You are on a journey of character development to become more like Christ. The real focus in life is to love

God to the best of your abilities and then to love your neighbour as you love yourself. That is it!

Give yourself time to recover. I worry about women who rush from relationship to relationship. They could be missing out on some valuable healing and processing time. You could have habits that need to be addressed because they keep sabotaging your efforts to attain or maintain a healthy relationship. When you spend personal time with God, He gets the chance to mould you and shape you. He will renew your mind, give you the right spirit, the right attitude, and deal with emotional baggage. It would be foolish to rush this season of singlehood along. Not that we will ever be completely perfect, but we can be stable. We should work towards better.

Your hope does not originate from past experiences, neither your current situation. Your faith is in God's Word, which details His promises to you. Find them in the Bible and underline them. Write them out on postcards and stick it around your mirror. Save them on your phone and flick through them on your morning commute. Keep His promises at the forefront of your mind because they are sure. Every day your faith can get used up as fuel and therefore has to be renewed. When your faith tank is full, it prevents you from becoming HOPEbroken. Once you are free, do not go backward. Push forward towards your bright future.

HOPEbrokeness can wear your faith down to a small little spark. Some of you have been through things that make you question whether you still want to follow Christ. I want to tell you that if a mustard seed can move a mountain, a spark can start a forest fire. Just a little faith will save your life. We all get weary with the pressures of life. But the Bible tells us... we win in the end.

Consider 2nd Corinthians 4:8, which says: **We are pressed on all sides, but not crushed; perplexed, but not in despair.** HOPEbroken for a moment, but God can fix it.

Psalms 147:3

{God} Heals the broken-hearted,

He binds up their wounds.

Chapter THREE

_____Myths_____

Myth: A widely held but false belief or idea.

Not that I cared about politics growing up, but I remember the tag line of a former English prime minister called Tony Blair. He was the one that joined hands with George Bush to invade Iraq under the suspicion that they had weapons of mass destruction. His campaign motto was "Education, Education, Education." Today I stand in front of a microphone, connected to stadium speakers, and cry out loud: "Education, Education, Education!"

Prevention is better than cure. This book explores both, but the spotlight MUST be on prevention. As a Doctor, let me tell you there are some preventable diseases. There are some mistakes you DO NOT have to make. Should you recognise the foolishness early enough, you can point your feet like a ballerina and step OVER the drama! Who wants to keep their heels clean?

I want to actively and aggressively tear down the notion that the *only* way to learn something is through experience. While we may individually have a preference for how we acquire knowledge, it is not possible to learn everything we need to about life through experience. Life is too short, and God is also wise for you to be stumbling around. The Bible tells that God orders the steps of a woman in 'right' standing. You are guaranteed to encounter un-avoidable challenges, but pick your battles when you can. You tell me not to drink that liquid because it is poison, I will not touch it if I have two working brain cells in my head. I will not run outside the road in traffic because it is dangerous.

Have you watched a crawling baby? At that stage of life, the parent has to have eyes in the back of their head. Every single thing, nasty or not, the baby comes across; they will put it in their mouth. They are learning about their world by taste, handling, basically having a personal encounter. That is what babies do.... Our learning styles can evolve now; we are women. Our

Bible tells us that we ought to flee from the very appearance of evil. You do not need to taste, handle, intertwine yourself intimately with the situation to appreciate it is not suitable for you.

You can learn vicariously through others and also study to show yourself approved in life. When you find a source of Godly wisdom, drink from it. Most people trust doctors, yet these health specialists do not experience every disease before prescribing medication that will heal. So, where you find advice in alignment with Biblical teaching…. Pay attention!

I do not deny that there are some lessons you will not learn unless you go through it yourself. Lord knows I was a tough headed child, so I can completely relate. God may allow you to experience some trials to shape your character and your faith. However, I believe that a significant percentage of the mistakes we make are simply a product of not listening to good advice—my stubbornness to learn contributed to my poor decision-making. Even when I suffered the consequences, I still did not want to hear, and so at the next opportunity, I stumbled headfirst into the same situation. You will find that destructive patterns in your social life repeat themselves until you grow out of it.

Why waste life taking the harder path? When you are healthy in emotion and spirit, you go out of your way to seek peace. My desire for you is to get through singlehood in good health. Who wants to be HOPEbroken? Not me! Every day I am STILL learning how to guard my heart better for out of it flows the issues of life. What I allow to settle in my heart affects my everyday life. There comes a time in your journey where you take charge.

Let me say it like this: to be successfully single; you have to put in as much effort into yourself as you would in a relationship. A number of us may not get married, so we should be ever-developing and living the most extraordinary life. You have to read, train, seek counsel and advice to be the best you for you. It just so happens that becoming that spotless, wrinkle-free, blemish-free bride of Christ will cause you to be the best version of yourself. You will become a strong foundation, which a good man will find great joy in building a family on. Curves and makeup may stereotypically attract a man, but the character will keep him.

Free your mind

My favourite movie is The Matrix. If you ever hear me speak, I will try my best to shoe-horn in a Matrix reference. It changed my life. God spoke to me through that action-packed science fiction adventure. The Matrix references start right now, and I am so excited about it.

I recall a scene where Morpheus is preparing Neo for his destiny. During a training exercise, he takes him inside the virtual world to the top of a skyscraper. He jumps across from that roof to the roof of another building across a wide road. Impossible in the real world, but Morpheus demonstrated that in the Matrix reality, it was possible. His advice to Neo was to free his mind. In this dimension, everything he knew before would be a hindrance to him jumping over. Old rules, old ways of thinking, things that belonged to his past were no longer relevant to his present circumstances.

If you want to avoid avoidable HOPEbroken scenarios, you are going to have to *free your mind*. I can think of at least four roots where negative thoughts about singlehood are created: Our fallen world, the people around us, our past experiences, and our personalities.

Fallen World

This fallen world is set up to snatch your integrity. Remember the Satanic University motto? "Kill, Steal, and Destroy." That is the Devil's full-time job, and God has given him limited freedom and power on this earth to do what he wants. There is coming a time when his rule will be over, but right now, we are in a warzone. The Devil wants to mess with your relationship with

God at any cost. We are saturated with lies about our identity, who God is, our value, the way we ought to conduct ourselves as women. Hollywood tries to dictate when we should lose out virginities. You are drenched with sexy advertisements, pushing us to "just do it." The very music we listen to carry the undercurrent that we should focus on things that please the flesh because there is no God! The Devil would love us to believe that there are no consequences to our actions. If it feels good… You cannot see the apparent damage to anyone, including yourself, it is your right to go ahead and do it.

At this point, I want to say that we all were born into sin after Adam's fall. I included. I am definitely included. No one is born in right standing with God. And in our sinful nature, we could be susceptible to living any sort of life. Drugs, alternate sexualities, lying, hating people there are no different grades of sin. If we pass on from this world with sins unconfessed, we are in danger of eternal judgement. You may feel your particular sin comes naturally to you, but my Bible tells me that to enter into the Kingdom of God.... You must be born again. Be born again.

> To receive Salvation or to be saved, it means that you have repented of your sins. You have accepted that Jesus died for you and commit to follow Him as Lord of your life. It is a freewill decision. Once you believe it in your heart and confess it with your mouth. You have salvation just like that.

Jesus Christ came down from heaven; he was entirely God as well as fully man, born of a virgin. This is a mystery wrought by the Holy Spirit. He grew up and spent three years preaching, teaching, healing, mentoring before allowing Himself to be crucified on the cross. He did not sin, but He took on ALL your sins. God loved you so much that He offered Son to die for you. Jesus took the punishment that was for you, and in exchange, you now have the gift of eternal life.

If you accept Jesus as your Lord and personal Saviour, you have been set free. To as many of them who received Salvation, He also gave them the power to become sons of God. (A position related to inheritance rather than a reference to gender.) Once you are saved... The Spirit of God dwells in you. You are dead to sin and now made alive to righteousness. As a new woman in Christ, you may still struggle with the temptations of the flesh and your former life, but you have immense power in Christ to overcome. You are who He says you are. Be born again.

As a child of God, you must appreciate that you are in this world but not of it. You walk and breathe in this earthly realm, but you have a soul and a spirit that belongs to another. You recognise the Almighty Creator as your good Father, and you live by the laws and precepts He has outlined in His Word. When Jesus ascended to heaven to sit at the right hand of God, He tagged in the Holy Spirit. The Holy Spirit is our guide, our person who helps us survive in this fallen world. All the fullness of the Trinity is in Him. He is a person, not a wisp of smoke or a force like the force in Star Wars. He has a personality. He is a person, so He speaks, He listens, He corrects, and He helps us to pray. He points out right from wrong, shows us truth where the Devil tries to twist it, and you need Him. He will help protect your mind from the fallen world that surrounds you. Jesus overcame the world so that you can make it.

Once you decide to follow Christ, it is a start, not the end of a journey. You are saved, but sanctification follows next to be a faithful follower of Jesus. Sanctification is where the Holy Spirit cleanses you of your sinful past, habits, attitudes, addictions, and behaviours. The aim is to become more and more like Christ. You may have heard of carnal nature, where you live according to how to please your flesh. But your divine nature is allowing God to shine out to the world through you. Your mind needs to be renewed after being saved. The Word makes mention of washing with the Word. We believe the Bible is the expressed thought, words, and heart of God to us. Reading it, understanding, following it, being challenged by it, and being changed by it sanctifying us. We will not attain perfection, but we grow from glory to glory, pleasing God with our everyday choices. It is a journey that we all share; we fall, get back up, and walk on with God. One day we will be glorified with our heavenly bodies until that day we press towards our goal.

Friends and Family

We all have them... well-meaning friends who will love dearly, but do not possess the wisdom of God. These friends can influence how we think about ourselves as a single woman and will impact our singlehood experience. Peer pressure is as rife in our twenty/thirty/forty hood as it is in the teen years. If everyone is doing something, it becomes the norm; and the trend could conflict with God's will. You have to be very good at discerning the difference in quality between your sources of advice. There is safety in counsel, but Godly counsel. They mean you well, but you cannot follow friends if they are not living in a way that honours God. That is why it is essential to be plugged into the body of Christ. You need sisters in the faith, aunties, and mothers who can objectively help you reason the heart's issues well.

Past Experiences

As a single woman, most, if not all, would have some experience with the opposite sex. A crush, an encounter, a dare, a school boyfriend, a teenage relationship, and some of you would have been in and out of relationships your whole life. Every interaction you have had with a guy can teach you something.

Your own experiences are a source of learning and influence how you feel about men. Some girls grew up watching abusive relationships between Mum and Dad, so they may not be shocked by the idea of a boyfriend hitting them. You can learn the right things, and sadly you can include unhealthy thoughts towards love.

Women are reading this who are victims of rape, incest, and molestation. I want to acknowledge you and your strength. To go through such violence causes deep wounds, and I want to encourage you to keep shining. The enemy tried so hard to destroy you, but God is a healer. HE has the final say in your life. I am genuinely sorry you had to go through that experience, but everything you were destined to accomplish... you will in Jesus name.

If you have not acknowledged traumatic events in your history, I want to encourage you to seek counselling. I pray that God will lead you to a trustworthy support network, so the memories will not oppress you. You will walk in freedom from condemnation and shame. As I am writing, I am praying that the Holy Spirit will minister to you. Your past will not derail your future. You are beautiful, valuable, full of life, and potential.

Your DNA

Last but not least, this could have been mentioned first; it is our nature. There are some preferences/likes/ desires you possess that you did not learn, but it appears to be natural. There are some habits we have and world views stemming from our own individual personalities that influence how we behave as single women.

Through genetics and the environment, we evolve as adult human beings as unique as our fingerprints. We are all different in personality types and how we deal with social interaction. This decides whether we are resilient and develop high self-esteem. It determines how confident we are in being alone, how comfortable with guys we are. Each of us differs in our levels of sexual libido after we hit puberty.

And there you have it, four different things that can directly influence your self-perception and thought life as a single woman. I have oversimplified it because these categories can overlap. One of the main things you must grasp is that 'as a woman thinks in her heart, so is she.' The enemy wants to have dominion in your mind, so we have to wear our helmet of Salvation. We need to make every effort that our thoughts are like the ones based in Philippians 4. Pure, noble, praiseworthy, lovely, and of good report.

Ephesians 4: 22 – 24 – (amp): Strip yourselves of your former nature[put off and discard your old un-renewed self] which characterised your previous manner of life and becomes corrupt through lusts and desires that spring from delusion; And be constantly renewed in the spirit of your mind [having a fresh mentality and spiritual attitude] And put on the new nature [the regenerate self] created in God's image. [Godlike] in true righteousness and holiness.

Your dating life can only be transformed by the renewing of your mind (Romans 12:2)

Time to Dispel the Myths

If one is to grow in their maturity within singlehood, one must identify the myths. When we are thinking correctly, we can benefit from socialising with men. Whether your ideas about love came from the media, church, your mother, friends, etc. We must sort truth from the almost truth. Some unhelpful thinking patterns will hold you back in your love life. It will undermine the practical reality of Gods' Word.

Writing this chapter was liberating. Even though I started this book back in 2011, there was no way I could have finished it back then because I had not grasped these concepts yet. I believed some of the following 'widely accepted facts" because they appeared to be true. However, after further inspection, I found half-truths, a myth or, in some cases, a flat out lie. Wrong thinking distorted my perception of myself as a single woman, and it did not make singlehood appealing. I wanted to escape this season of aloneness every day. But this has changed because I now have clarity.

MYTH 1

The reason you are not married is that God is still working on you.

Oh lord, if being in a relationship was an actual job, I imagine I would be overqualified. I have done almost everything to make sure I am eligible. There is a subculture in the church that says: *The reason you are still single is that God is still working on you.* THIS IS A MYTH. It is a half-truth! It is anecdotal. It sounds good. It resembles an encouraging word, but it also causes stress. It gives a single woman something to fuss over as she tries to get all her ducks in a row.

What happens when all the ducks are in a row as far as you can control things, and you are still single? We got awesome women in their 50's like Lucy, who desire to be married. They have high-powered jobs and properties; they are active in ministry, volunteer, work out regularly, dress well, good hygiene, ambitious, hard-working, funny, and cook to Michelin star standard. Their homes are well organised; they are financially secure and can recite Genesis to Revelation. YET.... They are NOT married.

How can you casually suggest to Lucy, a settled, confident mature woman past childbearing years, that God is still working on her? That there is something potentially so dysfunctional and immature in her that it would destroy a marital relationship? But Shenise, who is 32 and happily married, got married at 22, barely out of college. She could not boil water or toast bread. She was eyeballs deep in student debt and does not even attend church regularly. Yet she is happily married to a good man.

Do you mean to tell me that Shenise reached the golden status of 'ready for marriage' before Lucy at 22? No one is perfect, but come on!!

Telling people that the reason they are single because God is still working on them I know comes from the right place. You want to say that there are benefits and purpose in the waiting room. However, many interpret this to mean they are not "good enough" or "mature enough" to handle a relationship. It is not as helpful as you intend it to be. It enforces this celebrity status of married couples. Marriage is viewed as a prize available to those who have "qualified."

God may be shaping their character, but it does not mean they are not eligible for marriage! If you told me, God is still working WITH you to accomplish His purpose. I would nod to that. God might want your full attention for an assignment, so this encouragement is more palatable.

I kept hearing this half-truth over and over again, but I observed what was happening around me. I concluded that you do not have to have all your ducks in a row to get married to a Godly man. A lot of married folks say most of your growth comes after you say 'I do.'

There is an element of truth in this myth, and I must dissect this thing carefully. My rationale is that God continually needs to work on us regardless of our status. The Word says that we will grow from glory to glory under the Holy Spirit's leadership. Daily, we have to crucify the flesh, deny ourselves, and follow Him. Every Christian should understand that sanctification is a process that readies us for ministry on earth and retirement in heaven.

You do not need to stress yourself out about reaching an individual level of maturity, so you can "qualify for marriage." Immature people get married all the time. God is ALWAYS going to be working on us, and He is not working on us so that we can get married.

Now I want to make it clear that I am not knocking preparation.

Preparation is smart. I said immature people get married all the time, but the health of their marriage is another discussion. One would hope that as you go through life experiencing all it has to bring, you acquire wisdom along that way that would be helpful in marriage.

You should be doing all those things Lucy is doing just because you want to live the best life you can, not only to get married. God is not just working on you to become a wife; He wants you to enjoy an abundant life regardless. Pay off your student debt so you can live debt-free and go on all the holidays you wish to. Learn to cook, so you do not have to eat out every night.

Your future marriage will benefit from all the preparation you have done emotionally, practically, and financially. You will find when you are more stable; you may be able to make better decisions in a mate. You know who you are, and you know what you bring to the table. When you can live independently, you can not be bought or easily impressed. You are more than capable of taking care of yourself. To a mature man of God... that is attractive. You are not desperate for a man, but desire companionship and to be a helpmeet to him.

I would like to emphasise that there are benefits to preparing yourself for marriage. **BUT YOU CANNOT EARN A FAVOUR FROM GOD**.

Every good gift comes down from the Father of Lights. You cannot earn favour!!! Favour is notorious for not being fair. It rains on the just and the unjust. So yes, Shenise can meet her boo at 22, even though she has not done everything that some people think she should have, before marrying. After Miss Lucy has taken over the world, she may still come home to her opulent empty house.

If you want to encourage a single woman, instead of saying 'God is working on you' (roll eyes slyly), say 'you deserve true love. I do not know why it is taking so long. Let me know if there is anything I can do to support you. You are doing the right thing; keep going. You may have to wait just a little longer, but God can provide for your need.'

Single ladies, we can become so obsessed with getting ready, but do we even know when we have reached? How does anyone know when we have concluded that 'qualified for marriage status?' There is no course, no degree, no certificate you can earn. Life is just not like that, so you have to trust God.

> You can learn to cook when you get married. You can learn how to do laundry when you get married. Together you can create a plan to handle your debts. You do not have to be absolutely perfect in every area. Work to improve yourself for your own benefit. Stop worrying about qualifying for marriage. Change your focus.

A male friend shared with me, 'it is not necessarily about how accomplished the woman is... it matters, but not at first. What attracts me is how she makes me feel.'

MYTH 2

God owes you a husband.

This myth burnt me. I will be very transparent with you. I used to feel like God owed me a husband. But in actual truth, He does not. In the other Christian books I read, the women will never admit to feeling entitled, for it is not the saintly way. But you know I am not perfect... I felt God owed me.

I used to oscillate between two mindsets towards singleness. I have had times of retreat, where I did not socialise at all. I closed down dating website profiles and jumped in headfirst into my career. These were seasons of stillness where I was alone with my thoughts. But there were other times when I made time to socialise with the opposite sex. I dated purposefully. I believe you should experience both as a single Christian woman. There are lessons to be learnt on either side. What should be consistent is your desire to please God in all that you do.

Personally, I am striving to live a holy life. I am genuinely in my heart of hearts trying to love God and walk as uprightly as possible. It feels like balancing spinning plates on a pole sometimes. Each plate represents a different area of my life, health, spiritual development, family relationships, work, etc. At times, I can get them all spinning reasonably well. Whenever a challenge arises and threatens to topple one plate, I focus on it. When that is stabilised, I move to the area that needs more attention. I have accepted that I am not going to get everything perfect, but I do the best I can. It is hard work, and I do it because I want to get the most out of life. I do it because it is what I owe to God for saving me.

I cannot and will not sit there like a big ole barney wasting my talents or slacking off, when I do not know how many years I have been allocated. I have to be who God told me to be. I believe that I am happiest when I am living in purpose. I now understand that I do not have to be on the mountain top to feel pleasure. I am starting to enjoy the everyday breeze on my face and the scenery as I run this marathon. I know God is invested in the relationship I have with Him. Although He allows it to be tested, stretched, and developed.

When we read Luke 11 it creates an expectation that God will give us exactly what we ask. Psalms 34:17 talks about delighting in the Lord, and He will fulfil the desires of our hearts. So from one perspective, marriage is my heart's desire. I pray on it. When the Word talks about speaking things into existence, I do it regularly. I look in the mirror when I declare what I want to happen in my life. I avoid talking negatively, for there is the power of life and death in my words. So when I say God owes me a husband, it is almost an audacious act of faith. I can whip out scriptures to support my campaign manifesto.

But here is the catch: **IS A HUSBAND IN HIS WILL FOR MY LIFE?**

We are promised that we can have anything and everything we ask for as long as it is His will. However, God does not owe us marriage. What Jesus did on the cross was inexplicable by human logic. Motivated by unconditional love, He humbled Himself and allowed His creation to murder Him for their sins. We cannot ever repay God for His love. Presenting ourselves a living sacrifice and obeying His commands is our reasonable service.

We gain so much as children of God. It is a position that comes with inheritance, assess to the Father, and relationship with the Holy Spirit. Every Abrahamic covenant promise becomes ours through faith. We have the reassurance that God will provide for all our

NEEDS. However, our WANTS are negotiable, for He is not required to do anything out of His will or ultimate purpose. We have free will and can make choices, but we have no right to think we can manipulate God into doing something that is not in His will or not a need for us.

NEEDS	WANTS
Things we cannot live without.	Things that bring us happiness, comfort and benefit but we can survive without it.
Food, Shelter, Social relationship, salvation (Oh yes! I am minister of the gospel), health, protection, peace.	Disposable income, marriage, popularity, car, holidays,

I asked FB if sex was want or a need. Check out what they said. What do you think?

○ Varies for each person....neither is necessarily wrong'

○ 'Depends if you was made with a high sex drive or not.'

○ 'Sex is a want love is a need.'

- 'Married = need .... single = want to be fulfilled in marriage (the right marriage)'

- 'Good question, depends who is asking. For most men: sex is a physical and biological requirement. Therefore a need. The same could apply to some women. For some women sex is an act or demonstration of love. Therefore a need. The same could apply to men. Depends how the person is wired. 😊

- Oh come on saints stop playing games you well and know its A NEED!!!! 💦🔥🖤🦵😏.

- 'I'd like to suggest that needs have levels of importance. Anything can be a need, WiFi and general hygiene is a need. Food and water is also a need. Whereas I can live without the former two, I will die without the latter. Will a marriage survive without sex yes, will it be a good marriage perhaps, perhaps not. As others have said it depends on the couple....

- 'I would say it's just slightly more of a want than a need. If you are a single Christian you may 'need' but you can't fulfil that 'need' and have to ask God for help. If you are married, like someone said before, there may be a reason why your spouse is not able to fulfil the sexual side of your relationship but you can still have a happy and fulfilled marriage.'

I believe sex is a want for single people and a need for married folk. That is my perspective; as you just read, many hold their personal views.

The thought that God does not owe me a spouse is a challenging concept to grasp. Because it seems that ungodly prosper, they seem to get a lot of what we want without even acknowledging God. While as children of God, at times, we appear to struggle to get what we need. It is almost unfair, but God is sovereign. He is God and His ways. His thoughts are higher than ours, so we will not always be pleased about things we see in our lives and around us. You soon discover who is a disciple of Christ and who is not when prayers seem to go unanswered. Do we love God for what He can give us or for who He is? Many people come to the faith, and are disillusioned about what being a child of God is all about. It is not all roses and sunshine.

A scripture in Ecclesiastes 9:11 knocked me for six when I read it. God shows favour to whomever He wants to.

[Ecc 9:11 NKJV] 11 I returned and saw under the sun that--The race [is] not to the swift, Nor the battle to the strong, Nor bread to the wise, Nor riches to men of understanding, Nor favor to men of skill; But time and chance happen to them all.

What if you are one of those women who, for whatever reason, does not get married? What are you going to do? Will you stop loving God? Would you turn your back on your faith altogether? Do you believe you will ever experience pure joy again? Does the thought deeply worry or devastate you?

God does not owe you a husband for good behaviour. We ought to live right because we are saved. We need to be examples of Christ for those who do not know Him.

Sigh with me because this was not a myth I wanted to bust. If a husband is not in God's will for your life, you do have the choice to do your own thing. You can go ahead and get married anyways, but there may be consequences that you did not expect. God is concerned about your soul, your purpose, and your eternity. If having a husband is going to impact those two things adversely, He may say not my will. God is not jealous in a sinful way, but He is jealous OVER us and does not like to share His glory with another. It would appear that He does not OWE us... but He may BLESS us. It also may be a case of 'not right now' rather than a flat out 'no.'

Oh, to be blessed by God. I cannot imagine what it will feel like to meet someone that God has approved for me. Someone that accepts and loves me for who I am is a man who is happy to come alongside me in the Kingdom. I would be so happy. There is a proverb that says hope deferred makes the heart sick, but a desire fulfilled is a tree of life. I would have so many more reasons to give God thanks.

I made a meme for my women's page the other day, and it said: 'I am just as happy as a happily married woman.' I suspect that is my truth on a good day. I would be ecstatic that God cared about me so much that he would make a dream come true. I predict that it would give me a boost of good feeling that would last a long time. Yet, they say that your level of happiness as a single person is your base, and after your honeymoon phase of marriage (estimated to be around two years), you go back to that base level. Marriage comes with its own set of challenges, highs, and lows. So my meme was not false. I suspect there is a celebratory testimony that comes from God answering your prayers. And that is what I want.

Being a Christian is not about what you can get; it is about what you give. I keep quoting this scripture because it is so relevant and essential. Jesus said that those who follow Him ought to deny themselves, pick up their crosses, and follow Him. It is not just about God being your Santa Claus or fairy Godmother. Your love for Him must run deeper.

I tell you this, though, putting God first, seeking Him first; you will find that all other things will be added unto you. Those who seek Him with full commitment may find that favour comes to them. You cannot out-give God, so if you offer yourself a living sacrifice, prioritise Him, serving and loving Him. You can't lose. Somehow, someway God is going to blow your mind with His goodness.

The way we measure success has got to change. We compare our lives to those we follow on social media, not even appreciating the fact that we are not getting the whole story. People may look like they have it all, but cannot even sleep at night—no peace, no satisfaction, depressed, secret addictions, doing things that shorten their life span. Digital media dependency is likely to be recognised as an actual mental health illness soon. Many of us spend too much of our lives hooked unto social media; we are obsessed with seeking validation and projecting an idealised version of ourselves.

Success is knowing God for ourselves, walking with Him, living out the purpose He has for us, and making it to the end. We are not all going to be millionaires; we will not all be married; we might not get everything we want. But God will take care of our needs. He will make us laugh. He will give us testimonies. He will carry us through impossible times. He will destroy the plans of the enemy. He will fight for us. He will love us unconditionally.

In Christ, we find everything we need. If you can make Him your source of satisfaction and contentment, you have won in life. That is a success. Paul said in whatsoever state I am in, I have learnt to be content. LEARNT. He implies that it was a process; your process may take time.

I am not disputing the benefits of singlehood, but there is purpose and benefits of marriage too. Both please God when we do them well.

So just to make sure we are all clear, God does NOT owe you a husband. He can take care of you all by Himself. The only thing He will not do is meet your sexual needs in a natural way. Go figure. But as a singleton, a lack of sex will not kill you since it is not a need. We will speak more about this in chapters to come.

I am going throw this out there. There is something to be said about persistent prayer. There is the persistent widow parable, where she received justice for her case when she refused to stop harassing the judge. One thing I know about God is that He works at His pace. Perhaps He is looking to build your faith through persistent prayer. I have also noted in the Word a couple of times where it seems as if God changed His mind. (Exo 32:14, 1 Sam 15:11, Jon 3:10) It is always in the context of Him showing mercy to His children. From our human viewpoint, it appears as if God sometimes changes His mind, but what if He is taking us through a journey of maturation through persistence?

Another thing I know about God is that He is all about purpose. If He leads your life in a specific direction, there is a purpose to it. Even though it may be lonely and challenging at times, His heart is to bless you. He will cause you to prosper and to give you an expected end. I will repeat this: You cannot lose when you put God first.

My advice would be to acknowledge the low mood days; by all means, go through the valley but do not make it your home. You get through tough days by reminding yourself of the promises of God. You seek to make your life enjoyable, squeeze new experiences out of every day, and be productive. Continue trusting God to provide someone in His timing, but if He doesn't, we will have a remarkable life regardless.

MYTH 3

Marriage will complete you and keep you happy.

Someone needs to press the bell because we are getting off at this stop! Whoo... there are books written on this subject, so I am not about to go that deep. My area of specialty is singlehood, but let me tell you this now, marriage cannot make you happy or complete you. If you think that, you are deluding yourself. You are setting yourself up for disappointment and turmoil. You are putting on bags of sand on your arms and legs and attempting to complete a triathlon.

If you are not happy now, you are unlikely to be satisfied as a married woman. Your husband will not be your Saviour or reason for existing. I acknowledge the role a husband has in pleasing his wife, cultivating her, and leading her into new experiences. BUT HE IS MANNNNNNNN.... Human... He did not design you; therefore, he cannot complete you. He cannot heal you; he can only support in your process of healing. He has his own set of issues and emotional baggage for Jesus to manage.

You cannot depend on your husband to undo a childhood of traumatic incidences, to resurrect your self-esteem, or to rid you of every feeling of loneliness. He will not be there all the time. As amazing as your future husband will be, he is human and therefore flawed. He will not get it right all the time. He will commit sins, and what then? You both will encounter challenges that rise like giants in your face, and he may not be able to fix it quickly. For some women, they feel their life purpose is solely to be a wife and mother. It is an incredibly important role, but you need your own identity. When things do not go as planned with your family, your joy has to remain because it is fixed on truth anchored in God. You have to know who you are and be able to be confident in yourself apart from them.

It is reasonable to drag yourself as "half" a person into a marriage with a "whole" person. If something is missing or fundamentally wrong, marriage will NOT fix it. All it will do is bring that defect to the surface. It will expose those deep things that need God to heal. Marriage will bring out the real you. You cannot keep pretending forever. Something you both did in courtship; you both may struggle to sustain in a marriage every single day.

After the excitement and fuss of the wedding, after people have finished liking your honeymoon pictures, here comes real life. And sometimes everyday life is average and predictable. Your spouse is not a performing entertainer. He will have his job, purpose, habits, and hobbies to be getting on with as well as being your partner.

Psychologists say that the honeymoon phase, on average, lasts about 18 months to two years. Then your relationship starts to mature. After you have had sex in every position, imaginable things may not be so exciting and new. The next thing is a crash course in your partner's flaws and nasty habits. What was once tolerable and cute may become annoying and repulsive. This is where love comes in as a commitment to serve each other no matter what.

Voddie Baucham has a neat way of defining love. I hope I remembered it correctly: *Love is a conscious act of the will, that is moved on behalf of its object. It is not led by, but neither is it devoid of emotion.* Bad boy definition. That is the reality of real love, as the Bible defines it, not Hollywood. It is not based on Greco Roman mythology, which suggests that you can be infected by love. It can just happen to you, so you cannot be held responsible for your emotional attachment. Love is not what happens to you; it is what you decide to do.

1 Corinthians 13 expands on what real mature love is. The reality of marriages is not found in reality shows, romantic comedies, or social media couples. In real life, marriage is not just about sex, but it requires

maturity, intimacy, and honesty, among other essential things for success.

If you think marriage is going to fix you or make you happy (when you cannot even make yourself happy), you are in for a rude awakening. You must learn how to make yourself happy independently. The late Dr. Myles Munroe (miss him) would say that 'you are not truly single until you are whole...' You may think you are ready for a relationship, but if you have overlooked the fundamentals of a successfully single person, it is not good news for a potential relationship. As you read this... pause... think, if we use the definition Myles Munroe provided, are you genuinely single? Are you whole? Are you content?'

If the answer is no, get the yellow marigold washing up gloves on and get to work. Partner with God, listen to what the spirit is saying, and surrender to His process. He is working on all of us. As I have said before, we do not have to be perfected, but it makes sense that we reach some maturation before attempting to be a helpmate for someone. That person should not be expected to carry you through life. It will break him, and you will never be satisfied with his performance. If there are things I can do to help my future marriage, I want to do them.

I want to be happy, whole and fulfilled now to get the most out of my marital union. I want my foundation to be reliable to manage my husband and the everyday craziness he may bring. I want to be an independent competent person that chooses to co-exist with another independently responsible person.

Of course, I will be affected by all my husband does, but my joy will always come from God. My life may be shaken sometimes because I am joined with another person, but my joy remains as I draw from my relationship with God.

Marriage can put you in such a vulnerable position; you may not know how your man will respond to the challenges you meet in life. Woman of God, because you would have taken the time to stabilise yourself in God, you are enabled to stand next to him, flat-footed and weighty in faith. I can see you now... confident, focused, and ready to meet any storm head-on. You are going to be his partner, not his child. There may be times he is weak, and you have to minister to him. Do you have enough oil and wine to pour in? Yes, you do, because you are single, whole, and stable.

Myth 4

There is an expiration date after 30.

There is no expiration on getting married. Someone I know is getting married for the first time at 62. So just chill with the time pressure. Surely it is better to wait for the right one. I want you to have a happy life before and after marriage. I have committed myself to love myself well. I have realised that life is better single than joined to the 'wrong' person.

I refuse to progress a relationship that I know is not right for me and end up ruining a considerable segment of my life. Even though people treat divorce like it is nothing, in the life stressors scale, it is up there with the death of a spouse. It is a life-changing, tumultuous, emotional, and spiritual event. The financial and legal matters can result in devastating consequences. Of course, people come through it, but I am sure they would not recommend the experience. If you rush your decision on a life partner, you may end up in a tough situation.

We all know that there seems to be a marriage boom from the mid-twenties or so to mid-thirties. It is a popular decade due to couples completing higher education or settling in their careers. Like me, you may have to wait, but it is not because God does not love you. Your love story may just take longer to write. We will be fine. Your friends getting married will not impact what God has promised to you. There are too many people on the planet, and you just need one. Godly men will not one day run out. You are not in competition with anyone else, so do not feel less than, because you have to wait.

Quality, established, attractive single men roam the earth, and many are looking for women like you. When well-meaning friends say you should settle for someone who does not share your faith, do not listen to them. When people approach you with discussions of diminishing fertility, tell them to mind their own business in the most polite way possible. You do not have an expiration date on your forehead. When you walk hand in hand with Christ, you will be like the best wine. You become more exquisite with time. Ferment baby... one day that bottle will be opened. What a day of celebration it will be worth the wait.

If you never get married, the world will benefit from your maturity. Your presence is making a significant difference in this world. Recognise that you are a gift, and you are not up for auction. Because you may not have experienced many potential suitors vying for attention, you are not renegotiating your value. There is a high price of reserve that the King of Kings has set. You belong to Him. No expiration or best before. We reject that myth in the mighty name of Jesus.

Myth 5

Marriage does not work.

Yes, it does.

It is not just about a piece of paper.

Even if it was, money is a piece of paper; but people sometimes work to their detriment to obtain it.

God ordained marriage.

He was the one that determined that it was not good for man to be alone.

He brought Eve to Adam.

Marriage mirrors the relationship between Jesus and the Church. (see Ephesians 5:22 – 27)

Marriage brings out mature qualities in you.

Marriage was built to raise Godly children.

Marriage builds community.

Marriage builds Kingdom.

You are not a statistic.

Do it God's way.

You get God's results.

That is all I am saying about this myth. It is a lie from the pit of hell.

Marriage works.

Myth 6

It just happened...

Oops, I did it again, slept with that guy- it just happened. NO. I can confidently say that for women, nothing just happens. Single people, consensual sex does not just happens. Be honest with yourself.

Sexual stuff can feel so good that it becomes addictive. Your flesh is not saved even though your spirit is; your un-surrendered flesh wants to take every opportunity to get a fix. You may not have to go looking for trouble; temptation will find you. God bless you, ma'am if you are blessed to have a low to non-existent sexual libido, but for most of us, this area of our life is fiery and unrelenting. The myth I want to dismantle is the ridiculous thought of it just happened.

> Please note, that I am not addressing those who are victims of sexual crimes in this section. Rape, harassment and molestation is a heinous crime. If you have ever been sexually assaulted. I pray for your healing and peace restoration. I pray that justice will be served to the offender. God is a righteous judge who will vindicate you. Speak your truth and do not ever suffer in silence. Please see reference (3) in the back for help and advice.

Participating in consensual sexual activity requires a conscious decision. You would have considered the possible outcomes of placing yourself in a tempting situation. We women can be very intuitive, and a lot of us can pick up when a guy is sexually attracted to us. He may not even want a relationship with you, but sexual attraction is there. Their verbal and body language reveal their interest.

So we plan for the meetup or date, we know what could happen even if we are not sure. We wear the best underwear we have. We know if he drops us home and that late car conversation goes on into the night what might happen. When he touches your thigh, and you let that hand linger, you know full well what you want to happen next. Your flesh tells you to live in the moment and go with the flow. And boy does our hormones know how to flow! In these consensual scenarios, the guys will go as far as we let them. The men try it because they love sex, but sometimes we let them because we love it too.

Being single is crazy because we tend to have these sexual desires, and there is no legitimate way to fulfil them without sinning. If it is ok with you, we will go into more depth in another chapter. This is just a little dip in that big pool of complexity.

We cannot continually get ourselves into compromising position, hold one finger up with a sorry look on our face and say to God, it just happened. It did not. Even if you drank alcohol to the extent you lose your senses; you are responsible for that state of disinhibition. You know that if you drink that amount, you find it hard to control your carnal impulses. You are guilty and entirely responsible for any actions you take. It just happened needs to be crossed out of handbooks. More accurately, we decided to do x y and z because we were feeling horny, curious, or both. Say it like it is. You cannot address what you will not admit.

Myth 7

I am the only woman abstaining from sex.

You are not the only one. People that are not even Christians abstain from sex for lots of different reasons. The culture in the Western 21st-century secularist society is designed to encourage hedonism. They used to say that as long as it does not hurt anyone if it feels good, do it. But I think sexual sin hurts a lot of people, including yourself. It is not sinning when enjoyed in a heterosexual marriage, but something God gave gifted to mankind for procreation and bonding a husband to their wife. However, the way the Devil works is to pervert God's plan. I believe the number one rule in Satanism is 'do what thou will.' Whereas Jesus taught us to say not my will, but the Father's will be done.

The norm for society is to lose your virginity in your teenage years. As 16 is the age of consent for sex, some people view that as a target. You are considered "frigid " if you choose to keep your legs closed. Love became harder to find because sex became so available. It is women who set the terms for a sexual encounter. Back in the day, there was one approved way to get the 'goodies.' But now, pushed along by an extreme feminist agenda, women did not want to be married before they engaged in sex. Other factors led to this sex-crazed world, which I will not get into now. However, our attitudes toward sex have been heavily influenced by secularists.

Some women fear that if they do not add sex to the mix, the guy will just move on to the next woman. And he just might. There are plenty who have sadly deceived themselves into thinking that sex is just a form of exercise. They encourage you to have multiple concurrent sexual partners, threesomes, orgies, dominatrix experiments, and not be labelled as anything abnormal. You are heralded in society as a liberated 'free spirit.' But this hedonistic lifestyle will not satisfy you. Short-term fixes attempt to cover up genuine needs, but it does not work long term.

You were not designed by God to use your body as a plaything. The sin may seem 'fun' to the flesh, but these physical highs are shallow and fleeting. There is a way out of sexual immorality, and we will discuss it in a later chapter (Chapter 5 Healthy Sexuality).

I find the double standard between men and women intriguing. It appears to be okay for men to sleep around, and they will hang with a 'free-spirited' woman. But when it comes to settling down and getting married, they do not want the kind of woman they used to pursue. They want a 'nice,' innocent girl with a good reputation. I think that is crazy!

Mature Christian men seek out women who abstain from sex. Not boys now. Mature Christian men. They take pride in knowing that their woman has guarded her body. They are looking for someone who will reserve intimacy for the one she intends to be with for the rest of her life. *(I am not saying if you have a sexually active history, men will overlook you. If you have left an immoral lifestyle in the past, it is behind you. You should not be judged for it.)* Whatever your history, your present lifestyle should be consistent with your professed faith in God.

This whole thing about having to be well experienced in bed on your wedding night is a load of Hollywood hogwash. So what if the first couple of times with your husband is new and a bit awkward? When you get married, you will have the rest of your lives to have fun learning and discovering each other sexually. Just because he may have practiced with other women does not mean that it will work for you. I want to dispel the stigma attached to being a virgin or one who has abstained from sex in singlehood. As long as you two prioritise sex and communicate as a couple, you will learn how to satisfy each other.

To be honest with you, abstinence has become more comfortable for me the older I have become. I made decisions to avoid social situations where I would be tempted. I avoided entertaining men who told me that they were sexually active and interested in sleeping with me. Perhaps with fewer opportunities and the fact you get used to not having orgasms. Abstinence then becomes a usual way of life. When you first pass your driving test you, you have to focus on every action you make. The more driving experience you build up, the more subconscious the process of driving becomes. It takes some initial learning, testing, and then experience. If this is your area of weakness, my suggestion is to learn how to manage it as a top priority. Sex can complicate your perception of what a good marriage potential is.

It does not matter who else is sleeping around; sexual sin is not for you. Be comfortable with the fact you do not obey the norm. This world would have to believe that your sexual impulses cannot be controlled. That you have a right to have sex and that there are no rules. This is not true. The Bible admonishes us to be not conformed/ assimilated/ aligned/meshed in/apart of this world, but be transformed by the renewing of your mind. (Romans 12: 1-2) As Christians, we live in the world, but we do not live by the same moral standard, and our value system is different. Once you give up your virginity or you break your abstinence, it is significant. It does matter.

God WILL forgive you in a heartbeat; that is why His son Jesus died for you... Please see 1 John 1:9. However, you have to recover and heal through the consequences of intimacy with someone who is not your spouse. God can and will restore you when we make mistakes. Be encouraged that we have the power to choose a lifestyle of wholeness, health, integrity, and peace.

A significant proportion of women who lost their virginity, regret doing so in the manner that they lost it. Buzz words I have heard over the years: Curiosity, peer pressure, STI's, love pressure, unwanted pregnancies, used for their bodies, physically underwhelming and emotionally void. My prayer for you is that you will honour your body as God does. The Holy Spirit has chosen to reside in you. Sex can never be just a physical thing, and I discuss this further in a later chapter, 'Healthy Sexuality.'

Maybe you are like me, a technical virgin. Done things, but not the whole thing. I think it is debatable to draw the line as to where sex begins? Words? Kiss? Kissing with tongue? Touching? Hands stuff? Mouth stuff? Where is the line? My advice to you, if you are a technical virgin, stop, do not go any further. If you have lost your virginity, stop! Don't go any further. If you are in a sexual relationship. STOP. You do not have to go any further.

Wherever you are, God can help you maintain your virginity and restore you to purity. Let us reason together, and though your sins may be as, scarlet God will make them white as snow. Even if you have a history of sexual immorality, God loves you. He can and will forgive you, transforming your life forever.

He is a compassionate God; His love is not to be taken for granted. Even if your sin is great, His love is greater. Never give up on yourself because God will never give up calling you. Answer Him. You do not have to fix yourself or change yourself to come to God. Just start talking, He is listening. He is the one who will help you if you let Him. You are one of His precious daughters, and He desires you to be respected, whole loved, and holy. You belong to Him, not to these men who promise everything and deliver nothing. He wants to give unconditional love that outshines any physical sensation. A temporary orgasm will not validate you or satisfy the soul. It will not be enough for you as you require more from life. Sin always takes you further than you want to go, keep you longer than you want to stay and cost you more than you want to pay.

You are not alone. There are a bunch of other women who are in the same position. God is proud of us when we choose to honour Him. He can provide a husband that will cherish our heart, body, and soul. The most important is that the Holy Spirit lives inside of us, as our bodies are considered temples of the Holy Spirit.

It is possible to abstain from sex, do not let anyone lie to you. No, it is not convenient if you have a naturally high sex drive; but you can do all things through Christ that strengthens you. It may be more than you can bear, and that is fine. Let the Holy Spirit take some of that burden. Some things are humanly impossible, but that is because we need the Holy Spirit to empower us. He will not fail you, even if you fail Him. Get up. A righteous man falls seven times. Holy Spirit will enable you to get up. You are not your mistakes. Get up, go on and sin no more.

Myth 8

Divorce means you cannot marry again.

Divorce is a contentious issue that I am sure has caused church splits. Some singles had to survive awful divorces, but they have also been ostracised by religious folk. People who misuse the scriptures to oppress and control have perpetuated dogma that you are not allowed to remarry under any circumstances. The scriptures they refer to is Matthew 5:32 and Matthew 19:9.

In Matthew 19:3-9, Jesus teaches that there are biblical grounds for divorce. Sexual sin and desertion by an unbeliever are not the only way someone can forsake his or her covenant obligation of marriage. Abuse of any kind is biblical grounds for divorce as the husband has broken the covenant expectation to love his wife as his own body. (Ephesians 5) No woman should be expected to remain in a marriage where she is being tormented and injured. God is too merciful to allow this of his beloved children. Yes, there is the potential of reconciliation after the character transformation of the abuser, but people should be supported in leaving violent hate-filled homes.

I remember how the Pharisee's threw that woman, who was caught in the act of adultery, at his feet. He had mercy on someone who had done the wrong thing. After saving her from a public execution, He told to get up, go on and sin no more. Jesus released her to live a better life; He gave her a second chance. Why would the same God that poured out grace on that lady not pour out grace on those who have been divorced? Whether they have sinned or not, there should have another chance.

One would expect those who have been divorced to allow themselves a season to heal. It is a life-changing event that can have significant psychological, financial, spiritual, and emotional consequences. I do not advocate people who are separated or legally separated to date. It is better to close one chapter of a book before opening another. I encourage friends to engage with counselling, therapy, the Holy Spirit, in achieving closure. Divorces can create heavy burdens that can crush subsequent relationships if not released.

If you have been divorced, there is hope that God will provide for you. You will know when you are ready. Never married singles, you can marry someone who has been divorced; however, you should make your decision on a case by case basis. There are non-biblical reasons for the divorce as well. Explore what happened from different angles if you can. Is there a pattern with this individual in how they deal with conflict and the challenges that come with marriage? Is this person a born again believer and living according to God's word? If it is appropriate, do they take ownership of their decisions? What will they do differently with you? Is there a real possibility that they may reconcile with their ex? Time is your best friend, so proceed very cautiously. Seek wise counsel from people you trust and, of course, pray for God's direction.

Myth 9

You should not pray for a husband.

There is this weird, weird, bizarre thing that I have heard. Some people are actively discouraging single women from even asking God to provide a spouse. As if praying for a husband somehow means you love God less. But it is NOT wrong to pray for a husband or have an idea of what you need in a future spouse. Praying for wisdom regarding dating is necessary to date well. You can still be sold out for Christ and desire to be married at the same time. God cares about your love life!

When purchasing a property, most buyers will have requirements. You will have ideals and non-negotiable features the property has to have. There will be some things you cannot compromise, but other luxury features you can live without. It is usual to through a lengthy thought process when buying bricks and mortar. Yet, there are ill-advised busybodies do not believe you should have any opinion on the man you will share your life with. I say speak to God about what you think you need, and how you will recognise your spouse regularly.

Your future husband, whoever he is, is walking, talking, breathing on the planet right now. There is no reason why you cannot start praying for him now. My Bible tells me to pray without ceasing. In Matthew 7:7 (and Luke 11:9), Jesus tells us to ask so that we can receive, to keep seeking so we can find, and finally knock so the door will be opened. There is enough theological ground to ask God for what we want and to keep asking until we receive it. Unless God tells you no, you have every right to petition God for your husband. Why not? In the unlikely scenario that marriage is not in His will for our life, God will tell you. It would be cruel of God to allow you to keep talking to Him about something He is not going to approve. It is not in His nature. So feel free to present your dreams and desires to your heavenly Father.

> Pray over your future husband even if you have no idea who he is. Touch on his prayer life, his health, his family, his career, and his ministry. However the Holy Spirit leads, pray! The prayers you stored up will manifest favour and strength in his life. It is like making a spiritual deposit into the marriage.

I would ask that you examine your list of desired attributes in your future spouse.

- ➢ Are you expecting reasonable things from the man? (Must be a millionaire or he is not the one)
- ➢ Are you asking for qualities that are based on the Word? (Does the Bible identity this characteristic or attribute as important?)
- ➢ Is what you are praying for necessary for the health of your marriage? (He must be able to fix a car)
- ➢ Are you offering something similar? (What are you bringing to the table?)

➢ What are your preferences? (Looks, height, bank account etc.)

There are non-negotiable things. For example, I will not for one second seriously consider entertaining a man who has not accepted Jesus as Lord and saviour of his life. I cannot be under the leadership of someone who has no relationship with the Holy Spirit. For me, I need more than the basic church attender. I need a man matured in the faith, a man who is going to challenge me and help me to be accountable in my walk. I desire a man who can wash me with the Word of God. A man who is walking with God and means heaven as his home. We need that synergy when it comes to Kingdom business. That is a non-negotiable for me.

Some women are particular about things such as physical attributes. Of course, you need to be physically attracted to the man; but that attraction can develop as you discover this man is everything you asked for. Let us be clear, though, hear me good. Please do not *marry* someone you are not physically attracted to, though, or you are asking for a difficult marriage. I have friends say he has to be such and such tall, this eye colour, six-pack, beard. Ah... those things are not as important as character attributes. You run the risk of missing out on the person God has for you because your idea of an ideal type is far too narrow.

God could package everything you need unconventionally. I hear the stories about how some women met their absolute everything on the list guy. He was everything they wanted physically. However, they later find out that the character of the man was awful.

I do not know why a woman would turn down a good shorter man but chase after the tall guy who treats them like trash. I know where my priorities lie, and it is not some social media couple that looks perfect according to Hollywood. I want someone who makes me feel happy after I close the social media app.

Please be prepared for this man to be four-dimensional. He will come with issues, flaws, habits and baggage that you did not ask for. You have them too, and he has to deal with you. There is NO perfect man. Let me bust that myth within a myth. He is a person with a past, present and future. Be prepared to learn some stuff you maybe did not want to know about him. He is not a gourmet burger, so he may be served with more than you ordered. Keep praying. Pray sincerely, pray continually, and pray with your list.

Myth 10

There are No Good Men Left.

We need to examine and make sure we understand what a good man is before we say there are no good men left. Everyone has their idea of what human perfection is, but sometimes we expect things from the opposite sex that are unreasonable.

Social media (if you are on it) heavily influences our aspirational goals. Couple goals this, couple goals that, then the press is pushing out the hot new couple. Oh, there is a power couple over there and this famous couple we know over here. A lot of the things that are promoted as aspirational are not even vital for a healthy marriage. What we are looking for may be based on traumatic experiences, or we may be attracted to things that are not good for us. We need to make sure that we are basing out criteria for a spouse on biblical principles and practical compatibility issues.

What does Biblical guidance look like? Well... the Bible says that we need to be equally yoked (2 Corinthians 6:14). It implies that the two people in the relationship are both followers of the Lord Jesus. Both must accept Him as Lord and personal saviour of their lives. That is the starting line; the foundation and God's heart is clear on this. We can choose to use our free will to go against this, but there is a rationale in God's principle. Proverbs says, 'how can two walk together lest they agree?'

I do not advocate missionary dating! If the Holy Spirit does not draw them to Christ, convict their heart and open their eyes to the beautiful Saviour... why would you be able to? You cannot save anyone. You could not save yourself. It is the complete miraculous work of Christ. Be friends if you can manage to maintain boundaries and protect your expectations. You can plant the seeds of the Gospel, but the genuine transformation of being born again is the work of the Holy Spirit. Pray for them earnestly as their salvation is most important.

But Sara Jayne you say, I know it has worked out with some many people who committed to someone who was not saved... the guy got saved later. I would answer them and say for as many people it worked out; there are many more who would say it was a disaster. The divorce rate is now around 60% of all marriages, in fact, worse in the church.

The Bible implores us to begin with the right foundation for marriage. Both single individuals *must* have a personal relationship with God. Maturity in Christ is another discussion, but the starting line is... has this man committed to Christ? Is he living a life led by the Spirit of God? Does he use the Word of God as his pattern for life? If the answer is no, it is unlikely that God is joining you to this person at this particular time in their life. Salvation trumps marriage.

Marriage is restricted to life on earth; there is no marriage in heaven. God is more concerned with where this person will spend eternity than who they marry on earth. Our life purpose is not merely to make yourself happy, but how can I achieve the mission of God in the earth?

Marriage is challenging enough, partnering with someone who cannot even agree with you in prayer is adding to the pressures marriage will bring.

Some of you may be dismissing guys with great potential because they are not fully established financially. My Mum met my Dad when he was between jobs. Let's say; they are sitting comfortably now. :: cue in manic laughter:: There is a way to distinguish between a worthless man who talks big and does nothing; and a man who talks sense, plans well, works hard and succeed.

1) Look at their track record of achievement. What has he done in the last 5-10 years that showcases his ability to follow through?
2) Look for the stability in their relationships. A man without mature friends and family roots is worrying. Secure relationships and a support network are essential.
3) Look at their relationship with God and their level of surrender to His will. Does he listen to God? Is he obedient? Does he possess wisdom?

A man with potential will have encouraging answers in these three areas. The list is not exhaustive, and you do need to hear from the Holy Spirit as to whether to proceed. It is not just about a man with money. A number of these fine men who have the big bucks treat their women like accessories. Not everything that glitters is gold. They may have a lavish lifestyle but not the respect for you that you deserve.

As I said before, there are good men everywhere. God knows where His sons are, and He capable of providing options for you. When you live a life yielded to the presence of God, we believe in His timing. I always smile when you talk to couples that knew each other for years before getting together. You may have met your significant other already. Life is funny like that. So do not pressure yourself to find a husband by lowering your standards. Pressure yourself to explore new things in life, meet lots of people, go on adventures and be grateful.

It does not matter how many men are in prison, gay or unavailable... you need just one out of how many billion. Reject that worry that may come when you consider the fact you have such few choices. See it as fewer opportunities for distraction or engagement with the wrong man. You serve a God who called something out of nothing, and He can provide for you.

Myth 11

You cannot help who you love.

WRONG. Love, is not an infection, remember? *Real love is an intentional act of the will, that is not void of emotion, but it is not led by it.* So all those people who say they fell in love with the person in the first moment they saw them, most of the time they fell into lust. These are the kind of people who fall out of love just as quickly. I am sure there are some exceptions, but they are in the small minority of relationships.

There will always be an element of faith when marrying someone because you cannot know everything about him and how they will evolve. To make the right decision about whether they are compatible with you, you do need to find out a few things about them. To

175

commit someone blindly is quite foolish and I do not know how else to put it.

Today, society preaches Burger King 'have it your way' sermons. It seems that couples are less likely to put up with anything less than what they expected. It is not worth working through issues because they make divorce seem so easy. It is heartbreaking to see a 'how to get divorced' guide next door to 'how to plan a wedding' guide in a shop display.

God has given us wisdom for every situation we will encounter in life. He said if anyone lacks wisdom, to ask Him directly, and He will increase it. I pray for wisdom every day. I search the scriptures for nuggets of advice on how I should handle my affairs. Even non-Christians read Proverbs because Solomon knew what he was talking about.

So absolutely yes, you can help whom you love.

What you cannot help is whom you are attracted to in the first instance. That chemically-based reaction and emotional fondness can activate without your conscious say so. Trust and believe what you do next with those feelings is entirely up to you. Emotions can change and must change if the object of your attraction is inappropriate. Married man, child, woman, animal, relative... sounds offensive, but it is reality. The flesh is not saved; it is ungodly and wants to please itself. Therefore if you follow its desires and wants, you will end up living a sinful lifestyle. It can progressively develop in stages; a series of poor decisions that led to you wilfully committing to someone that God prohibited. To free yourself, you need God's help and to make a series of better decisions to break those emotional bonds.

Woman of God take responsibility for your thought life and actively guard your heart. You cannot stop men from approaching or pursuing you, but you choose who you entertain. You decide whether to answer the call or to pick up. It is your decision whether you add the person on Facebook and spend hours combing through their photos.

Then there are times when we jump headfirst into a relationship that only exists in our minds. You do not know much about the person, but you feel you have a strong 'chemistry.' This person may have expressed interest in you but not commitment. So you fall in love with the idea rather than the reality. Good news, at any time you can wake up. You can walk away from confusing situationships. Do not let it steal your attention or steal your peace. There is a genuine connection coming. Allow your heart to remain unoccupied and available for the honest man of God.

How you date, and court has implications for how you approach marriage. Do not keep saying you are in love and dilute the significance of that declaration. Real love will not have you jumping from guy to guy. Recognise the difference between feelings, lust, attraction, interest and infatuation. You have to appreciate that real love is a choice, and it is unconditional. It is not based on how the person treats you and whether you feel in love. It a conscious decision to care for the man, to the best of your ability, till the day you die. That is Biblical love. Admit that you are attracted, and there is nothing wrong in being interested. But hold back from declaring love until you know enough about the guy to make that choice with your head and not just your heart.

There are various contexts of love, and there are different names to distinguish between them.

I am going on a detour now, but I would like to state that understanding and living out the Bible should be your number one purpose in life. My encouragement for you is wherever you think you are... Go deeper. The beauty of studying things in its original language is that it tends to be more descriptive. This strengthens the message of what it was trying to communicate.

For example:
Modern Translation: *I saw a bus*

The original version of a text: *I was peering down from a height and saw a large tour bus passing by.*

One has to study the Bible to achieve a more in-depth understanding. Holy Spirit is an excellent teacher. He had also inspired men to help us understand the Bible better. If you can learn Hebrew and Greek that is awesome, but if you are not able to; make use of commentaries, lexicons, concordances and other Christian resources. It will help you to juice all the nutrients from scriptures by excavating the original text. Research the purpose for and the context in which the book was written to receive additional insight.

We quote the King James version as the original text, but the original book was Hebrew/Greek, not English. And even the King James was not translated from the Aramaic language it was translated from Latin texts. I want you ladies to challenge yourself and get deeper, to interact with the Word. It is alive, and it will speak back to you when you ask questions and pursue answers. If you peel back the superficial, the Holy

Spirit will reveal truths that will enrich your life. He will help you connect the dots and understand the heart of God.

Let us now hone in on *Eros* love. The romantic love between a man and a woman that the world is obsessed with finding.

Eros – to be "in love" is to experience a state of emotional exhilaration, excitement or euphoria.

A feeling of being "in love" is not in itself a solid basis for marriage. Neither is "we don't love each other anymore" a basis for divorce.

There is a difference between being in love and being committed to love somebody. Then there is a matured love that develops with experience.

"For deep love to persist and grow there must be a giving relationship similar to that described in 1

Corinthians 13, for most people deep and secured love comes after marriage, rather than before."

- Gary Collins (4)

I appreciate that some of you have had terrible experiences in relationships. And those that promised to treat you right let you down and abused you. The good news is that there is an unconditional love that God gives that will show you how to love others. It is the only example we can firmly stand on one hundred per cent and model our behaviour on it.

In Christ laying down His life for us, He teaches us that love is selfless (Matthew 16:24) The fact He died for us while we were yet sinners shows us it is unconditional. It is supposed to lead to a covenant relationship. There is a spiritual agreement that includes but goes beyond the wedding ceremony and an official license. There has got to be negotiation and sacrifice on both sides. The purpose is to serve the needs of the other person above your own. This institution was created by God and was to be built between a man and a woman.

To love someone is a conscious act of the will as opposed to being 'something that comes on you,' that you have no control over. It is a choice you make to take care of the needs of the subject. It covers a multitude of sins and takes on the qualities described in 1 Cor 13.

It is not something to be taken lightly, and that is why Solomon warns us in Proverbs not to awaken love before its time. I believe it was Adam's Love for Eve that led him to partake in the disobedient act of eating the fruit. Love involves you submitting to the other person, and if you choose the wrong person to submit to, it can be disastrous.

The world always dresses up lust as love. Lust leads you to the bedroom; love leads you to the altar. Lust puts its needs before yours, it might sound like: "if you love me, you will do x y z." Love says " I want to protect you, I want to wait, I respect your body more than my own." Lust is never satisfied. Love says 'even if you don't do this, I am here for the long haul.'

If the above description of love sounded too heavy for where you are in a budding relationship, you might be underprepared for marriage. When we seek romance without responsibility or commitment, we put ourselves in a precarious position, and we could topple out of God's will very quickly.

We need to make sure we know how to distinguish between a crush, lust, like, in Love and Love. You can very well help whom you love, but whether you *want* to is another conversation.

Myth 12
The One.

Now this myth is probably one of the most controversial I will discuss. I had gone back and forth on the topic; because there is more than one way to look at it. I ended up putting as a myth to accommodate the less popular but more useful perspective.

God gave us free will and because of free will we have options. That means on one level if you find a believer who is filled with Holy Spirit, decent, hardworking yadah yadah all the other good stuff, there is nothing stopping you from exploring the potential of marriage. Those who require a miraculous supernatural sign before they make any decision, may be growing in their experience with God. Matured believers who know the Word of the Lord, can tune into the still small voice of the Holy Spirit to guide them without a miraculous sign. They recognise that God gives them options, and they can make a well informed choice. As long as your intended, meets biblical criteria for a spouse they become 'the one' for you.

It makes sense to me because out of the millions of people on the planet, and it is unfair to say you have to find a particular person. And if you marry someone else's one... wouldn't that set of a chain reaction which would mess it up for everyone everywhere?

There is another view that God has designated a specific someone for you. They say God did not make three women from Adams rib bone and see who he clicked with, He created Eve and that was it. I will acknowledge that some partnerships appear to be divinely orchestrated by God. God wrote such a sensational love story, that to deny the supernatural aspect would be wrong. For some individuals, it matters very much who they marry. Their marriage has a particular purpose for Kingdom work. I think about God sending an angel to tell Joseph not to break off the engagement with Mary but to marry her. No other man would do to fulfil the messianic lineage prophecy.

God can reveal a potential spouse or supernaturally orchestrate love stories. I have heard some lists so specific that who could it be but Jesus when that person walks into their life. Some love stories have the hallmark of divine intervention. However, I think these occurrences are exceptional circumstances rather than a rule.

God may not provide a supernatural sign to confirm that the person you are courting is your spouse. What you will find is a settled peace once it is known that they fulfil the Biblical criteria of what a spouse should be. Holy Spirit speaks to many in still quiet voice rather than through an angel, for example.

I always ponder about the relationship which was supposed to be a meeting of two soul-mates but they get divorced; should God be blamed? No I do not think He should be, even in the exceptional arranged marriage circumstance. I believe that the two individuals can use their freewill to leave a marriage despite their marriage being 'formed by God.' I believe in the perfect and the permissive will of God.

God made a promise to Abraham that he was going to be the Father of a great nation and that He was going to open Sarah's womb in a miraculous way. As they became more anxious that God was not going to fulfil His promise, Sarah gave her maidservant Hagai for her husband to sleep with, thinking that God needed help. Hagai gave birth to Ishmael, but he was not the son of promise. There was drama in the household and so Hagai and Ishmael were sent away. God took compassion on them and gave Ishmael a special blessing.

God opened Sarah's womb and gave Abraham, Isaac just like He said He would. I would say that Isaac was God's perfect will but He permitted Sarah's free will as she tried to manipulate circumstances. Ishmael is representative of His permitted will. He is merciful enough to allow the best to be made of a complex situation.

I genuinely understand people when they say they married the wrong person. There is a myriad of reasons why that could have happened. However, God can help them turn things around. Their marriage is not beyond the saving grace of God.

I do not know about you but I want the perfect will of God to be manifested in my life. I figure marriage is going to be hard enough. I want God to be in the centre of the marriage right from the beginning. I want peace during courtship not anxiety that this relationship is not approved by God.

It is likely that you will meet many men that you are compatible with or you may have options. Like every thing else in your life, bring the situation to God in prayer and listen for His response.

You need to proceed with your eyes wide open; does this man lead you to Christ or draw you further away? Do you have peace within yourself or are you struggling to get the relationship off the ground at every stage?

Myth 13

I cannot wait any longer.

I was always told that God would never put more on me than I could bear. I was doing a 'Youversion' devotion program a few months ago and it set me straight. There are times when God does allow the burdens to mount up, but you are NOT expected to bear it alone. God expects us to go to Him for rest. Do not think that you can cope with the burden of being single alone.

There are times when it is ok to grab hold of your pillow and cry. That wave of sadness when you feel when a romantic movie finishes and you wonder what it would be like to be a heroine in your own life story. When you scroll down your news feed of social media and all these couples appear to be enjoying life together. Jealousy can creep in so quietly and its hard work making sure it does not set up home in your heart. Constantly battling your sexual urges and trying to manage your sexual desires is tough.

I broke down in tears one day because I was struggling to open a jar of pasta sauce while living alone in New Zealand. I often go out to eat alone, cinema alone, shopping alone and I desire intimate companionship.

You may feel like you cannot hold out any longer. You are emotionally exhausted with disappointment. You are tired of praying the same thing over and over again, and it feels like nothing is changing. Does God even hear you anymore? Does He even care? Then here comes the enemy with his lies dedicated to magnifying your weaknesses. You look in the mirror and you struggle to see a worthy woman, whole, healthy, beautiful, lovable..

My dear sisters, there are going to be good days and bad days. It might even last longer than a day, may be a week, it may be a long season. But the thing about seasons is that they change. As the earth rotates on its axis and spins around the sun, the seasons come and they go. God created time for us to measure and mark events. Weeping may endure for a night but I guarantee you that morning is coming. God will give you something to smile about.

The truth of the matter is that you can keep going. Do not hide your frustration and disappointment. Even when you are weak, that is when your Jesus is strong. He makes you strong so you can endure the wait. Please do not settle, sometimes we snap just before a moment of blessing in the same way that it appears to be darkness before the dawn.

Delayed gratification is an unpleasant uncomfortable term that people do not like. It is easy to demonstrate this principle with children. You might say I have 20p in my hand now, but if you wait till I go to the bank I will give you £20. The child is very likely to take the 20p because they can see it in front of them. Waiting requires their understanding that what is promised is worth more than what is in front of them. It takes faith that what is promised exists and will be given to them. They must have a security and trust in the relationship with the person who made the promise. It takes patience to wait for that delivery. Apply this principle to waiting for your future husband and you will not be side tracked by men who clearly do not belong in your life. The concept of temporary inconvenience for permanent improvement is a hard but life changing.

Myth 14

Nobody decent wants me.

If you think or feel that no one decent wants you... be honest. You do not have to pretend. Some of you may be frustrated right now. You feel that the only guys that show you interest are; the elderly, the immature, the financially destitute and the players looking for free sex.

As a woman thinks in her heart, so is she. So if you believe the lie that you do not attract good guys; that is exactly what will happen. The way you speak about yourself has power to influence your life. It is so important that you believe that you are valuable. You are special and capable of attracting a good man. No more negative talk! Say this with me: 'I will not talk myself down.' Your past does not have to be your future. You carry the power of life in your tongue. Make a habit of announcing the good things that are coming into your life.

I choose not to be irritated when 'undesirable' guys 'shoot their shot.' I consider it to be flattering. I am beautiful, I am intelligent, I am a good woman. They may feel they have nothing to lose but everything to gain if they approach me. It is not reflection of my worth but simply confirmation that I am 'all that!' I do not need to be rude or kill their confidence to communicate I am not interested romantically. How we treat people matters to God.

I think it is good to be firm but polite. Clear but not cruel! I thank them for their interest but make it clear I am not available. If they do not get the message, they are met with: 'Thank you for your interest but I am not comfortable with your continued pursuit. Please stop now or I will have to block you.' I am very comfortable with my block function. Life goes on.

The good men (that you are compatible with) may not know you exist yet. Simple as that! They simply have not met you yet. And if they know you exist they may not be ready to approach you. Let us not be double minded, we will be consistent in our faith. Now is not the time to settle or lower our standards. Be patient with this season. Be positive in this season.

Conclusion

Myths about singlehood cause much panic, worry, stress, fear and that is not what God wants for us. I could not possibly discuss everything but I hope it has challenged some misconceptions inspiring you to renew your thought life about singlehood. The war on

HOPEbrokenness starts and ends in your mind and so it is very important to focus on what is true.

> I leave the words from Philippians 4 with you.
>
> Finally, brothers and sisters, whatever is true, whatever is noble, whatever is right, whatever is pure, whatever is lovely, whatever is admirable—if anything is excellent or praiseworthy—think about such things.

Chapter FOUR

_____Mudholes_____

The definition of a mudhole.... is a hole filled with mud.
:: applause :: I bet you were not expecting that?
Google, as over the top as ever describes a filthy,
squalid, or detestable place. Have you ever been in a
field just after the rain? Imagine for some crazy reason
you have on some heels! You are balancing the best
you can on your mini-stilts, but no matter how carefully
you place your steps; your feet sink into the mixture of
dirt and water. It takes every ounce of strength to yank
that foot up again. I have been there, and my foot has
slipped out of my shoe.

The worst scenario is when you are stuck with nothing
to hold to, to help lever yourself out. Not a great
moment. Children love mud, but as adults, unless you
are a tough mudder athlete, you keep well away.
Imagine you are in a car or bus and its wheel is stuck in
a mud hole. Vroom vroom! You rev and rev, but the
tyre is not able to get enough grip on this slimy, sticky

substance to move the car forwards. Mud not only contaminates but it can stop you from moving from one place to another.

Allow me to put it this way: there are some everyday situations that a single woman can step into and get stuck. This chapter was written to make you think about the potential social debacles out there. I present particular types of men and dating issues that I have personally come across. Some I have mentioned before others I have not. You would have come across a couple yourself, and I guarantee that.

I hope that you can recognise what a romantic mudhole is and carefully navigate your way around it. If you want to stomp your way through it, at least put on wellington boots. It would make sense to protect your heart while proceeding cautiously because no one wants to be Hopebroken. These frogs will keep you busy and away from your real Prince.
The Substitute Mudhole

Have you ever met a man who you knew was not the one for you? You are incompatible for one reason or another, but you like his presence in your life. You guys get on so well, the whole world can see it. And inside you are burning up for some real love. It may not be real love like real meat, but this tofu boyfriend helps satisfy the craving. Catch my drift?

It is a well-known fact that friendship is the ultimate foundation of a happy and lasting marriage. We are told to marry our best friends. These things are right, but it creates potentially tricky scenarios that a clued up single needs wisdom to navigate through.

We generally connect with people we are attracted to; we may share similar hobbies or interests. We choose to spend time with people we like, and often we develop an attachment to them naturally. This attachment can take on a life form of its own and evolve into something that needs addressing. This is the perfect set up for developing crushes. Good for you if your crush feels the same way, but goodness help you if he does not. The crush accomplishes what was prewarned on the tin. You then have to deal with your feelings and expectations. All in all, it is not the most satisfying experience, and you can lose the friendship completely. It is something that can mess you up if you do not manage it well.

Throughout my life, I have attempted to make substitute boyfriends out of my friends. More often than not, they are physically attractive, and I enjoy their protective company when we went out. Most did genuinely care about me, but for one reason or another did not like me in 'that' way. It is so easy to fantasise about options when you know you do not have any in reality.

At school, I was the girl who when she had friends got on with boys better. They seemed to accept me for who I was. I was not one of the girls boys liked romantically, but I was funny. I enjoyed guy things like wrestling, superheroes and hip hop culture. They would make jokes about me beating people up for them because I had a larger stature. I never did, but I seemed to be the cool girl they wanted around. It was refreshing to be accepted, but I always had a desire to be a girl guys liked. Of course, the popular girls were most popular for a specific reason. I was not about that life then, but the attention and accolades they received was appealing.

The vast majority of my friendships with guys never turned out the way I thought it would. What would happen is that they inevitably would get a girlfriend and turn their attention in that direction. I would become insanely jealous, very hurt and withdraw myself from the friendship. I would compare myself to the girl of his affection. It was not a happy time, and each time it happened, I felt less and less confident about myself. When you are a child, you think like a child. The rejection was un-addressed and not noticed by the guys in question, and I suffered from a deep complex, thinking something was not right with me.

As an adult, I do not think I get on with guys better than girls. I get on with both genders equally. I have an extensive network of associates and acquaintances. There are a lot of guys I can hang out with and have a terrific laugh with. But intentionally do not develop close friendships with guys who I am not related to any more. I do not confide in them or spend lots of one on one time with them. This is because I know myself and protect myself with boundaries. You may be very different and quite happily have lots of close male friends, and that may work for you, but not for me.

I even make a distinction between a single male friend and one that is in a relationship. There is no way I want confusion created for his wife or girlfriend, so I am cautious with boundaries. Call me old fashioned, but I respect a guy who is working on a relationship. I do not call late, often and I don't hang out with married men alone. The Bible advises us not to let our good be spoken evil of. Flee from the very appearance of evil. Respect the relationship and keep your distance. If he would leave her for you, run a mile. Because if he did it for you, he would do it TO you. Emotional affairs are a real thing. It may begin very insidiously but understand that severe consequences follow affairs.

> If the guy is single, I ask myself
> Am I attracted to this guy?
> Am I confident in the fact that this guy just wants a platonic relationship with me?
> What does he bring to my life?
> What are our boundaries or would I do this if he had a girlfriend?

I have to be able to answer those questions on a regular basis, because as life happens things may change.

Allow me to reiterate that platonic friendships have boundaries. You should not treat your friend as your substitute boyfriend. If he flirts with you or does things that are confusing it is up to you to reinforce the boundaries. Do not go along with the flow, you do not know how many other women he is doing this with. Set yourself apart as exclusive because you are an incredible woman. As far as you are concerned, if the guy has not verbally expressed interest in you; it is absolutely fair to assume he has no serious interest in you. If that situation changes, he will let you know and you can respond to it as you please. If he keeps trying to mess with your emotions after you have confronted it… distance yourself. Being pre occupied with a time waster will leave you with regret.

How not to fall in love with Mr Substitute…Time restrict. Time restrict. Time restrict. Or restrict Time. Restrict Time. Restrict Time.

Do not be available and accessible to him on a 24/7 basis. Phone calls should be restricted to convenient social hours. Even if you are just watching youtube at 11pm at night do not take his phone call. I have this 10pm rule because I promise you many men's brains turn to mush after that hour. When they get tired they start chatting foolishness as their inhibitions appear to loosen. He could very well be in a suggestible (horny) mood because he is tired. It happens but it should not be your problem. If he is calling to pray with you, feel free to do so before 9pm. It is nice to enjoy the social chit chats but the phone call duration should be limited.

Permit the casual what app messages to go unchecked for a few hours. Quickly responding like you are holding a hot potato sends the message that you are too available. Treat him like a company who wants to discuss a phone upgrade with you. It is a conversation you want to have but only when it is convenient for you. Do not bombard with him with messages which could be seen as fishing for attention. I promise you he can smell desperation. Do not allow him to dominate or suck up your time. It is not about a power struggle. It is about keeping the boundaries crisp and clear so he knows and you know he is NOT your boyfriend.

(Fictitious texts during dating stage)

Him: WYD

You: ...

Leave him on read. Do not respond because grown men can text in full sentences. In the age of predictive text, there is no need for this lazy abbreviation. That's just my opinion as a professional woman. He will double text. Or even call to make sure you still have time for him. You are not someone to entertain him or cure him of boredom. You have a full life! He will learn.

Hey! I was just thinking about you... what are you up to?

You: Hi, trying to make some lunch. How is your day going?

This is how grown-ups converse. He may just want to let you know he is thinking about you and only have time for a small exchange. Keep it light; keep it fun, and keep it interesting. Do not pause absolutely everything to go into an in-depth conversation.

Him: You up?

You: ...

Nothing. You guessed, right. No, you are not up at the wee hours of the morning. This is a time where a lot of mischiefs happens. If he happens to be travelling, working late or the gig just finished. Speak to him in the morning. Do not respond. The next morning... 'Sorry I was resting... is everything alright?'

Him: Send me some pictures.
You: You can have my social media if you like. But I do not send my pictures out to guys.

If you are not on social media, then promise to arrange a video call at a convenient decent time when you have time to prepare. I get it, men are visual creatures, but I think it is creepy to send pictures during these times when you have alternatives. It is good to verify who you are speaking to, as some people post old photos. However, if they are requesting pictures to gawk at for me, it is unnecessary. If you are not in a relationship with them, do not allow it. I think it is a good thing to make your what's app a picture of you, but that is it. If you met them online redirect back to your profile. Your pictures. Your property. You do not have to send them yours. Some perves have the audacity request specific revealing photos. DO NOT SEND ANYONE sexual photographs or videos of yourself.

Have some mystery

I know you guys are friends but do not give up all your goodies for free. I mean your intellectual property, your hopes and dreams, your fears, insecurities, childhood memory. All this stuff is valuable information that should be shared with someone who you are intimate with. Once you have said it or sent it, it cannot be deleted or unsaid. Be careful not to give pieces of yourself away because this is an emotional process that can end up as an attachment.

It does not take a long time for an emotional attachment to manifest. The intense regular conversation will do it. This is why restricting your time conversing will guard your heart. They have to earn information about you through consistency over time. They must also demonstrate their trustworthiness. Have they disclosed some of their personal information to you? Do they refuse to bad mouth previous exes? How have they reacted to more superficial, less significant things you have shared? Judgement? Mocking? Joking? Shock? Is there a genuine interest in who you are as a person? Do not reveal too much too early. Have some mystery about yourself, and it will keep him interested.

Him: Tell me about your previous boyfriends.

You: I will when I am ready. They have each taught me a little something to shape me into who I am today. My last relationship was over a while ago. I have moved on, and I am ready for something new.

Physical force field

Physical touch is a significant form of communication. Seventy per cent of our conversation does not come from our mouth. Some guys are naturally flirtatious and use physical contact to build rapport. Make sure they do not get too comfortable with you. Sitting on a guy's lap, wrestling, napping together, hugging up. Stop it! It is a language of love! If this guy friend has not expressed romantic interest in you, why are you letting him do this? Where are the boundaries?

We want God to watch over us but not watch us sometimes, huh? So if it helps, imagine your Pastor is present when you are hanging out with this guy friend. If you feel uncomfortable with a particular form of physical contact with your guy friend in front of the Pastor, it is likely it is inappropriate. Or if this helps you, imagine another woman doing that to your man? Is it appropriate now? You might feel special at the moment, but it builds an emotional attachment that is difficult to break. Remember we are talking about how not to fall in love with Mr Tofu (sorry if you like Tofu, this is just for an analogy).

This is where we could argue about the role and nature of the male best friend. Be careful with these 'best friends.' Go through those five questions mentioned a few pages back and keep your wits about you. A woman may very well form a friendship with a man; but for this to endure, it must be assisted by a physical antipathy. If there is a physical attraction, you are asking a lot of yourself to be so close, to care for them and not fall in love with them. It is a coup that few women can pull off successfully.

How would you feel if you met another man and he did not appreciate the intimacy of your relationship with the friend? What would you do? Or... what if your future husband had a female friend that was his best friend? How does that make you feel? How would you deal with that? Can you see why I am picking at boundaries and being clear what a friend is? Most women would not tolerate their spouse using another woman as their 'rock' or 'confidant.' It is inappropriate, and exactly how emotional (than physical) affairs occur.

A male friend is simply a friend unless he SAYS otherwise. That means you need clear boundaries and a mutual understanding of what your friendship is all about. This may or may not require an open, honest conversation. You do not want to find yourself in a position where you have invested a lot of time and emotion into this male friend under false pretenses. You do not want to trust your life secrets to someone who may be seasonal.

A substitute is precisely that, something standing in the stead of the real thing. You do not want to be occupied with a substitute when the real deal comes. You do not want to be pushing a banger of a car when a Bugatti relationship comes along. Save yourself. Do not throw your future husbands treasure to someone who treats it as 'fool's gold.' Your heart is precious; you are a beautiful creation of God, full of purpose.

Let us flip this on its head and look at the other aspect of a "substitute situation." It flows very nicely. Your "friend" maybe your substitute, but perhaps he has made you his replacement as well. You are his appetiser but not the main dish. Let us explore this substitute/appetiser dynamic in more detail.

The Appetiser Mudhole

The unofficial warm-up girlfriend

Loneliness can be cruel, like a wintery breeze at night pricking your bare skin. It howls in your ear, causing your very being to shake. It rattles your heart like loose old wooden window frames. It can be hard to ignore as the chill sets in, and you will do almost anything to get warm. Anything will do, nearly anybody will do. Enter the unofficial girlfriend.

That was me... an appetiser. The food you scoff down before the main meal. I have done that... I played that role as if I was Will Smith going for an Oscar. I have been that go-to girl who will "hold them down" come rain or sunshine... for FREE!!

We run away with the idea that love is friendship on fire and never look back. DO NOT my sisters, I beg, do not be the appetiser. A dude will have no problem using you as a warm-up girlfriend. And then when he is ready to go after the woman he wants, he leaves you high and dry. After all, you invested in his wardrobe, even if you were his nurse, although you became Gordon Ramsay to feed him like a King. All your investment and dedication will become a return for his future Mrs. If you are friends, be precisely that, be platonic and stay in your lane.

In a lot of the friendships we have with the opposite sex (non-relatives of course,) the guy knows what you offer as a woman. He likes it (because you are friends,) but for whatever reason, you are not his full package. It is nothing you have done or have not done, so do not obsess about being anyone else but yourself. Set your emotional boundaries and check your expectations are based in reality.

> Reasons a Guy may not 'want' you.
> (This is to bring clarity to what can be confusing and challenging time.)

You are too high value for him. He cannot physically, emotionally, mentally or spiritually afford you. You have set standards that he is unable to reach or maintain. He can only keep up a pretence for so long. He then becomes unsettled until he made it clear that you are to expect no more from him than you would a friend.

He is not physically attracted to you. Unlike women, it is harder for a man to overlook physique. I am not saying there is anything wrong with you; you might not be what he prefers. Do not attempt to change yourself for a man. Best believe that you are entirely what a better man is praying for. Be you, love you.

He is immature and does not recognise who you are. Some guys do not see the qualities you carry even though it is under their nose. They are quite happy playing the field, and the idea of settling down has not even crossed their minds. You will never be good enough for a man who is not ready. Do not stress, be friends if you can handle it and understand that a mature man is coming.

Male friendships can work well when approached correctly because there is a lot we can learn from each other. Enjoy their personality, presence, and their perspective on life as it will give you insight. Hang out in a group and laugh it up. Be a supportive friend but also please keep your feet well on the ground. If you find yourself becoming jealous when he interacts with other women, your feet have left the ground. You do not own him or have the right to dominate his time or attention. Your emotional attachment will put your heart on a runaway train, and who knows what will happen after that? This is a vulnerable position YOU can protect yourself from.

There is always a chance with the genuine and mutually beneficial friendship that over time the guy does develop feelings for you. He could be waiting for a specific time/circumstance to make his move. That is the coveted scenario which may very well happen. However, until he does make his move, the principle should remain no wife privileges for zero commitment. (Double underline that!)

The move is not cryptic texts, him calling you babe, "a look," flirting, him being protective when it appears you were in danger. All these things are non-specific and subject to interpretation. This is precisely what happened to me. The man's behaviour was in the grey area between friendship and romance, but in his mind, it could be logically explained away as "caring" friend. A move is when they tell you. Out of their mouths shall flow words of real intention. That is when you can be sure they have a romantic interest in you. Your friend means well, but you cannot be sure what he wants until he speaks up.

If the "friend" you are dealing with is mature, they can very well man up and express their thoughts and feelings. If he does not say anything to you, it is either because he is not ready, or he does not like you in a romantic way. Make it simple for yourself and do not count your chickens before they hatch. I have learnt this from experience so you can learn from me. Anything can happen, and this guy may not be your husband.

Now if you are uncomfortable and fed up with their confusing-are-we-friends-or-lovers behaviour; then initiate a conversation to address it.

It would be wise to have a conversation in a public place (neutral ground) with semi-privacy. (Plan a separate route home just in case it is awkward and you need space!)

1. Be factual
2. Speak slowly like you are presenting an argument and keep your emotions in check. Emotional displays (crying, agitation, anxiety, desperation) become a distraction for men.
3. Talk them through why you are uncomfortable or fed up. If this person is your true friend, they should want to protect your feelings. If you say when you do

a b c, it makes me feel 345; he should understand that very clearly and wish to amend his ways.

4. Listen to exactly what he says and believe him.

5. Do not argue or become heated if it is a response you do not like. Nod and accept it. (Flip out later at home) Maintain your cool.

6. Respond honestly. Even if you do not know how to take what they said... just tell them that you need time to process.

7. Thank them for their time, and you will follow up.

Word of warning, he may declare that your friendship is just a platonic friendship and deny giving any confusing signals. If he refuses to take ownership of his shady behaviour, it speaks to his immaturity, and you are better off without him as your man. In another scenario, he may acknowledge the confusing behaviour. He may then explain that either he is not ready to progress or he does not like you 'like that.'

If you do not take rejection well, do not initiate an open discussion about your friendship. Instead, create distance between you and the "friend" for your peace of mind. Give your feelings a chance to detach from him. Force yourself to go over facts, which is; he has not said anything to you; therefore, he does not have a right to take over your thoughts and your heart. Take your heart back.

"The friend" may notice you are withdrawing from him, he may not; but stick to your choice. You are choosing to remain clear-headed and available for a good man that you click with but is also ready. As a disclaimer: you may lose the friendship if you choose to challenge their behaviour. I would question the benefit of having a male friend who inappropriately interacts with you and does not want to protect your feelings. Your first loyalty is to yourself. Protect your heart. Pull your heel out of the mud.

The whole "friends with benefits" thing is an ugly ungodly concept that does not end well for either party involved. It is a form of sexual immorality wrapped up un hedonistic self-indulgence. It goes against biblical teaching as it dishonours your body as the temple of the Holy Spirit. And quite frankly, you think you are getting what you want, but you are settling. Mere sex will not satisfy your real need. There is no positive benefit or sustainability in it because you deserve better.

We are hopeful romantics, and we pray that we find ourselves in the scenario where this long time friend becomes a lover. It is tough to suppress a quiet hope; especially when this "friend" is a somewhat decent guy with a lot of the qualities you are looking for in a future spouse. You calm yourself with maybe he will, if you can show him your best qualities, you have been through this together so surely he will notice you. It is as if you are in a never-ending audition. You may have a neutral facade, but deep down inside you are anxious for him to come around and recognise that you are his treasure. He may; he may not. But in the meanwhile, guard your heart. Just in case he is not the guy and you end up getting emotionally shredded when he pursues another.

You are worth too much to be an appetiser or a rehearsal. I told myself I do not run a finishing school for young men. It is not my job to teach a guy how to be a man, to take care of him and be that 'breast' when baby gets hungry. Do not hold down a man as a wife should. That is so beyond friendship.... If he wants all that access, support, nurture, and time from you... he needs to wife you. The right man will.

The Uncertain Mudhole

He does not act on his 'feelings', or he is inconsistent.

If a guy has expressed feelings of attraction to you but does not want a relationship... think about this carefully. You need to choose whether you wish to continue a friendship with him. You risk getting into a situation that is going to raise your expectations that might go unfulfilled.

When the guy of the hour is honest about his uncertain

feelings, believe him. Honesty is a sign of man, and it is reassuring that you are dealing with a considerate person. But do not make his honesty about his indecisive the main reason to wait for him to make up his mind. Do not wait. That is my advice. I think that if that man does not want to pursue a relationship, there is a good reason.

Do not push the pace. Let him sort his life out, make his life choices and decide to pursue you. Do not wait around; obsessing over him, it is draining. You will become occupied with the potential of a relationship and remove yourself off the market. But if the man is not clear about his intentions, do not commit to him, it is a mudhole. If you push him to make a decision, you are likely to push him away. You do not need to force your future husband to commit to you.

It is like a shopper in the jewellery store, admiring a piece. The sales assistant notices the interest and gets excited about a potential sale. The buyer finally announces I like it, but I am not ready to purchase. The sales assistant has not taken a deposit; he knows nothing about the buyer and watches the buyer leave. You would think the sales assistant is crazy if he took that jewel out of the display cabinet and put it in reserve for that buyer. It would deny the opportunity of a sale to another buyer—a customer who has the intention and resources to purchase that piece. The same principle should be at work in dating.

Even if you like the guy, if he does not know if you are the one for him do not take his vagueness, personally. Just accept what is and manage your expectations. Toss him back to the acquaintance or friendship pool. Be mindful though; he should not be exerting influence over who you talk to, where you go or what you wear. He has no rights. Nothing. He is an acquaintance or friend who has an attraction to you. Nothing more.

If he has told you that he is not ready for a relationship, do not give him the attention as a love interest. He does not get a reward or special treatment for liking you. Of course, guys will like you; you are amazing. Try not to lavish your love and undivided attention on him because he will take it. He will take as much as he can get from you because he likes you.

This scenario highlights whether you are comfortable in singlehood and self-esteem. If you are uncomfortable or your self-esteem is low, the attention will feel like ice cream in the heat of summer. Without much hesitation, you will find yourself falling in love with someone who is ambivalent about you. Not the recipe for a lasting relationship.

I never again want to be in a position where I have given my heart to someone who did not ask for it, deserve it, nor earn it.

Dear God,
I do not want to be careless with my heart. Some difficulties are unavoidable but some that are the result of a foolish choice. So Lord, lift a standard around my heart. I do not want to be easily accessible. I refuse to waste time, be distracted or abused. I want to be about my Father's business, but I can't do that if I am

continually nursing a broken heart.

The right man will find a wife in me because I will be in the position you have asked me to be in. My future husband and I will meet at someplace, sometime, somewhere.

God, even if I do not ever get married, I still love you and will rock with you till the wheels fall off. And they won't because Jesus is the wheel in the middle of the wheel.

The way I think has got to change and the way I feel will change after that. I do not want to be led in making decisions for my love life by my feelings. My feelings cannot be trusted in the early days of establishing a good connection with someone. So the Holy Spirit lead me! In that still small voice instruct me in how I should respond to opportunity. Please help me to recognise an opportunity in the first instance and also let me know when it is time to step away.
Amen.

The Passivity Mudhole

God will bring someone to me at the right time so that I will do nothing in the meanwhile.

Firstly, yes, I agree with your initial assessment of the Christian dating pool. It is abysmal. Depending on what micro-season God has you in during singlehood will determine the action you should be taking regarding your social life. There may be times God will ask you to remain still, focus on Him and a specific assignment. And there are other times He says be wise but go ahead, be proactive. There will micro-seasons of activity where He will provide prospects, and you need to walk out on faith. He will help you to navigate the dating world.

Some women feel comfortable with absolute passivity when it comes to getting married. They expect God to send their husband to their front door. (And it does happen!) So I am not going to say stop doing what you are doing if it is working for you. I would encourage you to take inventory of what you have accomplished in your life, and many things came to pass with partnership WITH God. You had to do something to act on the desire God placed in your heart. Overall, I think it is healthy to be active and intentional about your social life.

[Pro 14:23 NLT] 23 Work brings profit, but mere talk leads to poverty!

[Pro 6:6-9 NLT] Take a lesson from the ants, you lazybones. Learn from their ways and become wise! Though they have no prince or governor or ruler to make them work, they labor hard all summer, gathering food for the winter. But you, lazybones, how long will you sleep? When will you wake up?

So if all you can do is declare good things but not act on faith... do not be surprised if nothing happens. I instead work a job to save up money to buy a house.

God will show me which ones out of the ones I look at is for me. I instead act out my faith, then to forever spin around, declaring I want a house.

I do not even know what to say but to be honest with you, once I had healed from HOPEbrokeness, I went into idle Christian single mode. Passivity in singlehood is the prevailing culture in the Western World. I grew up with no one encouraging me to socialise. I was encouraged to everything else but socialise with good guys. Even though God inspired me and worked with me to accomplish amazing things... my love life was a place of slumber. I needed to wake up and walk out my faith. You may need to check-in and see if you are guilty of the same. I am just going to lay that question out there and back away.

NOW please hear me good! I am not giving you the green light to run ahead if God has you stopped at a red light. You may be in a 'time out' micro-season if there is a scent of HOPEbrokeness. If you date and you are not ready to... it causes problems. It can become so addictive to have guys flirt with you, compliment you, and there is an exciting rush of meeting a new potential. Some women fall in love with the process of falling in love, and marriage becomes mundane for them. The constant flow of social activity may distract you from vital preparation for marriage. So it is crucial you openly dialogue with God with what micro-season you are in. God will empower you to be productive in a micro-season of proactivity.

When the green light says go, what is holding you back? If you need support or practical advice on what you can do as a Christian woman to get started, I can help.

Check out my website www.adammeetevehere.com for more information. #Shameless plug. Boom there we go.

Mr. 'All Potential No Action' Mudhole

Ever charming but no substance

Guys are wired to be visual creatures, and I am sure you have heard that before. They are attracted to what they see in the first instance. Women, on the other hand, can be captured by what they hear. A guy you may not find that physically attractive can wear you down until you accept a date because of the things he says if he has any experience with women, he will know what to say and how to say it. This is just how it is and so sisters you need to be vigilant about what sweet nothings he is pouring into the side of your head.

There is a 'brand of man' who talks big and talks fast, but his words do not match his actions. He says one thing, but he consistently does the other. While you are in the dating phase if you find out inconsistency is his brand; take off your heels and RUN. You cannot trust a man like this to lead you anywhere in life because he either deluded or a liar. He may have lost touch with reality and genuinely cannot produce what he dreams, or he wants to manipulate you with deceptive words.

Here are some more questions you must ask in the dating phase that will help determine whether has potential. I mentioned in Chapter 3 under Myth 9. Spread the questions across conversations. You want to avoid turning the date into an awkward interview. Maybe ask during dinner and some over another phone call.

What are your life goals?

How are you pursuing your purpose?

Where do you see yourself in the next 5 years?

Is there anything holding you back?

What is your plan B?

Does he know who he is? Does he know what his God-given purpose is? How can someone lead you if he does not know where he is going. You need to know if there is a pattern of achievement or whether he makes excuses for not reaching his goals. Has life indeed dealt some challenges that would set anyone back? Or has he just been distracted? Is he self-motivated? What is going on with him? Does he believe that he has achieved what he needs to at this stage in life?

He may be satisfied with where he is. He may not want anything about his life to change except to bring you in. And if he is satisfied, you need to be at peace with where he is. You will have to accept whatever his situation is. So if it is a good situation great, but if it is a challenging situation... walk with your eyes wide open. You will not be able to change him. He will only change if he decides that change is necessary himself.

We went on a slight detour, but we are working back to the main point now. If a man is showing signs that he is not consistent in what he says and does... get out now because he is not going to change. Do not ignore the red flags because they will come back to knock you out later. This brand of man will lie about small things of no consequence. So trivial, you could almost laugh it off and excuse him. But he is showing you that a lying spirit oppresses him. If he will lie about something trivial... he will like about something significant.

Trust with someone new has to be built. It takes time to grow, and you need to observe their behaviour. If there is no trust... there should be no relationship. Do not build a house on sandy land. The truth is the only person that can genuinely change their character is Jesus Himself. Holy Spirit has to transform his life by sanctifying his mind with the Word of God. I do not feel comfortable at the idea of submitting to a man that does not like to tell the truth. Burn me once, shame on you, burn me twice shame on me because I kept proceeding through a red light. Burn me three times... nope, that is not going to happen.

Men are very good at telling a woman what they want to hear. However, what he does proves his character. For example, consider Roger (fictional), he continually talks to Laura (fictional) about what he will accomplish as a businessman. He speaks about the life he will live once he makes it. He says he has a plan, but it is not even written down nor has he approached anyone for advice. He is unemployed when Laura met him. Rodger has no viable career/business plan, and he is waking up in the afternoon to play video games.

He has not signed unto the job centre or offered his services to volunteer somewhere. For all his talk, he is not realistic or consistent with actions. He is not showing signs of being a hard-working, ambitious and mature man. He has not got a realistic plan of getting to where he says he wants to be in the next few years. Rodger very well may have potential, but flapping lips do not understand you what you want out of life. Laura needs to consider whether he is at a place in life where he can offer security.

When a guy speaks to you, close your heart in the first instance, but open your eyes and ears. Do his behaviour and actions match up with his words? He says I am ready for a relationship but then continues to entertain other women. He says you are the best thing since sliced hardo bread, a top priority yet he makes no time to spend with you. He may say that he is a good father to his children, but never spends time with or contributes financially. This is my problem with building a relationship with someone online or long-distance dating. You have little to no opportunity to peer into everyday life. It is crucial to verify as much as you can in the early stages of a relationship before you invest your heart.

No one is going to be the finished article; he may need a good woman by his side to achieve his full potential. But understand the risk you are taking by marrying someone's potential. The problem with potential is that some men will not reach their fullest potential. Can you live happily with that man if he never changes or achieves what you want him to?

Fall in love with the integrity, heart and personality of the man. What he says is what he does. He has a vision for both of you, and he is taking steps towards it. He is about action even more so than words. You can trust a man like this to take a leadership role in your life. These are the kind of men who are destined for success no matter the obstacles that get in their way.

The Missionary Dating Mudhole

He is not saved but...

Whoo. This is a mudhole. This is a mudhole. This is a mudhole. I spoke on this subject earlier in the book, but it is so important, we will revisit this. It is possible for missionary dating to work out in the end but most probably will not. It is not recommended. It is an incredible thing to evangelise and tell a loved one about the gospel of Jesus Christ. Evangelising to a man because you like him and dragging him to church, sounds praiseworthy but it can backfire. You will feel a false sense of security that this man loves your God when, in fact, he may just be acting the part to win you over. I do not encourage Christian women to start a romantic relationship with a man who is not a born again believer in Jesus Christ. (Has he accepted Jesus

Christ as His Lord and Saviour. Does he believes that the Bible is the final authority in life and submits to it).

It is one thing to be married to an unsaved man, and then you become a Christian. But it is an entirely different thing to start a romantic relationship with someone who does not know your God personally for themselves. It is commendable that he may be a "good person" but is he a God person? Goodness does not give access to heaven. It is not going to give your man the abundant life and power Christ gives us. Being kind does not provide you with insight into spiritual matters and knowledge on how to deal with the Devil. Goodness does not take away the fact that in reality, you serve two different masters. It is a foundational stone that will affect the direction of your life and future family.

Time and time again, I have witnessed Christian sisters date a non-Christian. They bring them to church, and the guy may or may not make a commitment to Christ. The moment after they are married, the guy feels he can relax. He has won the prize, and he stops attending church. His relationship with God was riding on his relationship with his woman. He attended to make her happy. If the man does not subscribe to the teaching of Jesus or consider God the head of His life, this is not a green light situation!

Your faith is not meant to be compartmentalised; Jesus lives inside of you. His light touches every part of your life. It matters very much who you bond yourself to. They can either be a blessing or a burden. Falling in love with somebody you know does not have their relationship with God may cause significant conflict.

How can your husband sanctify you with the washing of the Word if he does not know it? He is accountable only to himself rather than being responsible to God. What happens when God tells you to do something, and he does not agree? The love we ought to emulate is the love of God. Your husband should know of this love and experience it for himself to love you right. Living by the teachings of the Word provides you both with power, wisdom and example. You both can stand on this standard as a firm foundation and manage life obstacles.

I know that some horrible self-professed "Christian" men have dragged their wives through hell and back. I know that there are non-Christian men who have such kind hearts and have it all... but salvation. Despite these two things, we have to honour God in all that we do. Either we live a life in surrender and service to Him, or we do not. I'll repeat it, Jesus taught us, not my will but yours be done.

If you choose to put a man above God, you make that man an idol. God does not tolerate idolatry. The decision will impact the relationship you have with God.

I do not believe there is anything wrong with being friends with guys who are not saved. He may come to faith as a by-product of your friendship. This is different from missionary dating; this is being an active evangelist in your everyday life.

Live right, stand for Christ, share the Word with your friend and do invite him to church. Pray earnestly and fast for his salvation. Winning a soul for the Kingdom of God is an incredible achievement. (Although Holy Spirit does the convicting and saving. God uses us to bring a testimony of His love in sending His Son Jesus) Allow God to make a son out of him before you try to make a husband. Placing God at the centre of your marriage gives you that third-string to make a cord that is not easily broken.

I want to share you with something my mother shared with me in the last year or so. It is clear that I am spiritually mature; I have a bit of Bible knowledge and experience with walking with God. My mother released me from having to marry someone who is exactly like me. I mean, he has to be saved, but it is OK... if he is growing. Someone who has a genuine relationship but may not be on the same 'level' as someone who is matured in the faith. He may express his devotion to God in a different way to me, but he has a relationship that is progressing. He may not know as much about the Bible as me, but there is a hunger to learn.

Growers just need time and encouragement. I felt that someone who was not on my 'level' would fall into the category of 'unequally yoked.' But I believe I was wrong in my presumption. It is a delineation between believer and unbeliever, someone in the Kingdom of heaven and someone in the Kingdom of Darkness. Once he is a believer and he has made that choice to follow Christ, this is made evident by their lifestyle. Holy Spirit can do a work in him, which will amaze you.

My mother's advice made me relax just a little because the guys on my 'level,' the ones I knew in active ministry certainly did not fancy me. LOL... they wanted Melania Trump, not Michelle Obamas! The one's that were 'up there' in their ministries saw me as competition rather than help meet. So this helped me to be more reasonable in my expectations when dating.

The Love Hurts Mudhole

Love does not condone abuse

This pains my heart, but I felt that it was so important to include this in my first book. Every time I saw a patient come into the emergency hospital room as a victim of domestic violence, it affected me. I wondered how she ended up in her predicament. We patch up the physical damage but cannot heal her inner torment and suffering. More often than not, these women go right back into the arms of their abuser.

Some of you may have personal experience of domestic violence. Others may have grown up in a home where you witnessed or experienced it as a child. My humble plea is that you talk to someone trustworthy if you never confided in someone before. If it is in your past but still affecting you now, understand that you can heal. God can minister to your needs directly and work with people he has anointed to support you. If you are currently experiencing abuse, please get help before things escalate. (5) This is your one life to live.

No matter how impossible a better future seems, it is not out of your reach. There are services and people out there who will help you. You cannot stay in a place where you are emotionally, sexually, mentally, physically or spiritually abused. This is not what God wants for you.

God wants to rescue you from this ordeal, but you have to reach out and take His hand. It may seem scary to make the first step to leaving someone you once cared or still do care about genuinely. But true love does not hurt in this way. Let me expose the lie. The truth is real love heals and nurtures. God said in His Word that husbands should love their wives like their own body. A sane man does not harm and beat upon his body; therefore, there is no way no matter what you do that a man should even think about hurting you.

Abusive relationships appear to reveal itself insidiously. It never begins crazy like a frog sitting in a pan bathing in lukewarm water. The temperature rises so gradually, the frog does not notice, and it will not jump out to save itself from being cooked. Raised voices, heated arguments, slammed doors and punched walls. If the man you are interested in has anger issues, he is not safe to be in a relationship with. No matter how sweet and lovely he is at times. Life is one bumpy ride, and as humans, you are not going to get everything right. In a healthy relationship, you should be able to make mistakes without fear of being punished by your partner.

A man that hits a woman is troubled and weak. He is in demonic bondage if he feels he is justified afflicting pain on someone who he professes to love. There is no excuse, no exceptions and no circumstance where this is allowed. It is against the will of God, and it is against the law of the land. And vice versa women should not be abusing men... this too sadly happens.

When someone shows you who they are, believe them. Do not ignore anger and violence. It will not just go away or get better by itself. I have been around couples whose relationship smells toxic from a mile away. You can fool some people some of the time. But you cannot fool all people all of the time, and you for sure cannot fool God any of the time.

The person may very well get the psychological and spiritual help he needs to become a better person in the future, but your love will not save them. Your acceptance of their life-threatening foul behaviour will not fix them. It will only get worse until you decide to leave. I do not pretend to imagine the difficult decision you have to make, but this is a matter of life and death. Jesus today says to any woman in this situation... choose life! You may be scared of leaving but leave scared. God has freedom awaiting you. They cannot take away your hopes, dreams and destiny. You belong to God and whatever condition you are wanted alive. God has plans for a better life.

I once went on a few dates with a guy who eventually confessed why his previous relationship broke up. They were having issues, but the final straw was an argument that had escalated. He got up into her personal space and shouted at her: 'Do you want me to hit you?' He did not hit her. But they broke up. I learnt from that women's experience. He said it was his first time that he had been pushed to the edge. I asked him what he had done with his apparent anger issues; he said nothing. He said that he saw his parents behave in the same way growing up. At that moment, I knew he was not for me, for sure.

I advised him to get counselling and even found people local to him. I am not sure that he went, but a few months later I heard that he was engaged... scary.

People can change, but it takes intentional probing, counselling and spiritual work to get to the root. It is something that takes time and specialist support. I would not walk into someone's life to be their partner when they are going through this healing process. In the dating stages, it is rational to walk away because this is a problem that can cause future generations to suffer.

I do not think women go into a relationship believing their man is going to abuse them. But some things can be observed during dating/courting. I have listed some behaviours and traits to look out for, but the list is not exhaustive. They may be on their best behaviour for a long while in the initial phase of a relationship but keep your eyes fully open.

➢ What is his relationship like with his parents and siblings?
➢ Does he have a family history of domestic violence? If so? What support has he had in dealing with it?
➢ Does he demand to know where you and what you are doing all hours of the day?

- Does he seek to control many aspects of your life? (Fashion, movement, friends)
- Does he have a volatile temper?
- Does he have rapid mood swings?
- Does he have a history of violence and aggression?
- Does he speak poorly of your friends and family?
- Do your friends and family have concerns about his temperament?
- How does he handle disagreements between you?
- What happens when you make a mistake?
- Has he ever used his strength to restrain you? (outside of innocent play-fighting)
- Does he criticise your appearance?
- Does he speak to you in a disrespectful tone?
- Do you feel safe when he is angry?
- Has he ever touched you or come into your personal space in a hostile manner?
- Does he demand to know who you are talking to at all times?

➤ Does he look through your phone without your permission?

The way abusers work is by demanding control, and they use fear. You should not be afraid of anyone, especially someone who is interested in marrying you. Because they are insecure, they will break you down to build themselves up. When they chip away your identity, it is because they want you to be dependent on them. They will seek to separate you from friends and family. They want you to feel isolated and trapped, that you have no choice but to remain with them.

They are likely to speak badly about the people who have loved you all your life to create division and distrust. They want to be the only one you can talk to. These things are signs that the person is potentially abusive. Do not wait for more confirmation if you have an uneasy feeling or suspicion. Get out now.

People get the wrong idea about submission. They think it means that a woman is to allow a man to walk all over her. The man must control her without any respect for her feelings, preference or freedom. That is a twisted worldly idea of submission. Submission, according to the Word of God, is when you defer to someone. You permit them to lead you.

1. Submission, first of all, is only expected between a husband and wife. You do not have to submit to someone who is not yet your husband.

2. You submit to the man as they follow God.
If they are doing sinful things, you do not subscribe to that.

3. It is your choice who you choose to submit to.
If you submit to a coward, a fool, an immature man, he will abuse that position in your life.

In the same breath, the man is supposed to love his wife like Christ loved the church. Christ did not dominate and abuse the church.
Jesus submitted to God, the Father when He said not my will but yours be done. Through Christs' ministry, He said He only did what His Father instructed Him to do. One would hope if your husband is wise, he will listen to your

concerns and insights into a situation before making a decision. But anything with two heads is a monster.

The Biblical model of a family is husband is head, who covers his wife and children. God has the expectation of a husband and the responsibilities he has to fulfil. We have to prepare in our minds that there will be a transition from single independent woman to submissive wife. You do not give up your strength, but you defer to your husband's leadership. That is what it is essential to make sure you choose a man who is submitted to God. See how that works?

The behaviours and actions I listed above describe an unhealthy relationship. This is not love, no matter how "good" he can be. Those behaviours are unacceptable, and you ignore warning signs at your peril. You are royalty and deserve to be treated like so. You would not accept a plate of food with pooh in the middle of it, so do not take toxic controlling abusive behaviour in a relationship. It is far better to be alone and waiting for a better man. RUN. As far away as you can as quick as you can.

Holy Spirit will guide you in all truth. It is so vital you pray when you are investing time into getting to know someone romantically. You mustn't run ahead of the Holy Spirit. Listen to those who love you and who support your well-being. Friends and family can often see objectively because their heart is not involved.

Love does not abuse its object. It does not hurt. No matter what he has said or done, if you come across this awful behaviour, take it seriously. He will not change permanently because you ask him to or because you love him. He will only change if he is aware of his problems. He should be able to take responsibility for his actions, (i.e. it is not your fault) and face the consequence (legal action may need to take place). He is likely to require psychological and spiritual rehabilitation (it is a process).

Until then, a victim may find herself in a deadly cycle. He lashes out; she might leave, he expresses that he is sorry, promises not to do it again and is on his best behaviour for a short while. Inevitably, he lashes out another time, and the violence gets more severe and severe. This is no way for any woman to live. There is support to escape this kind of relationship.

Always Drama Mudhole

The struggle to even take off...

There is no smoke without fire. I am not one for perpetuating gossip and rumours. However, we live in a fallen world and a small Kingdom network in this country. If there are no safety concerns, I do not believe that women should 'warn' another woman about a guy they have dated. Leave them alone. Often the scorned woman is acting out of jealousy rather than kindness for the new love interest. If the man is rotten, the new love interest will soon find out.

I advise new couples not to tell the world that they are in a relationship until engagement. It is hard to resist the social media attention you get every time people post about a new relationship, but discretion is your friend (excluding accountability partners). I also believe that if your man comes with a negative reputation after YOU do some reasonable research, it may be a mudhole.

Social media is an incredible tool and aids communication between strangers. It can reveal peoples thought life, social groups, interests and hobbies. Do your research as well as you can when you are thinking about involving yourself with a man. Take what you find with a pinch of salt; not everything is as it seems, but it is useful information for later discussion. Even do an internet sweep.

Some relationships are a little bit harder to get off the ground than others. But surely falling in love should be the most relaxed and most natural stage of the relationship?

In the first stages, everyone is supposed to be on his or her best behaviour. If you find that you are confronting a lot of issues, having frequent arguments, dealing with one disaster after the next, I would say stop. Pause and question why these problems are happening? It is easy to tell the Devil does not want us to be together, but could God be allowing these things to happen to slow you down? Why are you arguing so much? Are you compatible with this man? Why do you have to confront ex-girlfriends? If you cannot find time to even spend with each other, is now the right time?

If your 'getting together' appears to be a series of falling out and making up, it does not sound healthy. There should be an enjoyment and peace in your courtship. Why are you going to bed angry every other night? A woman cannot live on drama alone. It is not fun. If there are too many skeletons coming out the closet... shut the door.

Sex Now Mudhole

True love waits

You do not have to provide access to your body to prove that you like or even love someone. No way! Nowhere! No how! If a guy is telling you he cannot live without sex; he is trying to manipulate you into bed. Sex will not keep a man. If you give in, you are likely to regret it. What feels good at the moment to your body, can upset your soul for much longer. If you have to sin to secure the relationship, God did not send this man to you!

Christians who profess to be born again and committed to Christ do not have sex before marriage period. I have a whole chapter dedicated to this topic, but to be clear in 2020, the Bible is still relevant. Abstinence may not be prevalent, but it is still the will of God. There are consequences to sin, and some you may just not want to pay. They are blessings that come with obedience, that are worth waiting for because God never disappoints. He is not a crazy God. He made sex and gave the conditions for it. Take it or leave it, but His word does not change no matter who seems to be getting away with it.

If you are not married and participating in a sexual relationship, you have stepped into a deep mudhole. It is hard to come out of because that physical and emotional high is addictive. I'll explain this in more detail later on, but sexual purity is not just about crossing a solid rigid line but a direction of the heart.

If he does not want to marry you, why does he get the benefit of a husband? Why should he enjoy the most intimate act you can do with another human without formal commitment? You are not a sexual plaything put on this earth to satisfy his needs. You were designed specifically for that purpose that pleases God. Sex is meant to be enjoyed with your spouse. It creates a special bond and at the appointed times brings forth children.

When you become sexually involved with someone, you are bonding to them as a wife should. Biologically your body adapts to his as you take on some of his genetic material. To be used for your body is not satisfying long term, neither does it make for healthy future relationships.

If this kind of a man wants to break up with you because you do not want to have sex, so be it. He is only looking out for himself and would not know how to take care of a queen such as yourself. True love does wait and respect your purity more than his sexual needs.

Sexual abstinence is a discipline that will set you apart from other women. Declaring your lifestyle early on helps you weed out creeps who are only looking for sex. Take steps to create boundaries and if he does not respect your limit... cut him off. Save your body for the one who will honour it, cherish it and who has committed to take care of it.

If you are stuck in this sex sinkhole, you can get out. Like some substance abuse, you will need to go cold turkey; there is no way you can just phase it out. I have spoken to women who have been very sexually active, and they do initially miss the feeling of physical intimacy. God helps you to develop coping strategies and restores your body mind and soul if you want to feel free to jump straight to Chapter Five for more information.

Refuses to Grow Up Mudhole

There is a difference between being a boy, a man and a man ready to be a husband.

Wow! The above statement from an old friend blew my mind a little. I think it is imperative that women who feel that they are ready to get married understand this. You must understand the difference between a boy and a man. A mature woman must never assume that because a man is of a certain age, he is indeed one with sophisticated qualities. Age is, unfortunately, a number.

So you will encounter a forty-year-old boy with a 17-year-old mentality, and you will also come across the 25-year-old who is indeed ready to be a man, the head of his household.

The table I have drawn up is an excellent start in highlighting the main differences between a "boy" and a man, but this table is not at all comprehensive. I hope that you will develop your psychological framework to see if the men approaching you are mature. Marriage is hard enough without entering the arena with a partner; you are not confident is ready.

There are several different categories of intelligence, so I am not saying all university educated people should go together and all people without A levels should stay together. But there needs to be a level of understanding, communication and compatibility between the two parties. It is more than an education. It is common sense, maturity, wisdom received from life experiences or competent counsel. You should not have to carry a fully grown man. It is unrealistic to expect a man with a boy's mentality to step up to lead you in life.

BOY	A Godly MAN
Afraid of commitment	Considers commitment as the goal of a romantic relationship
Overly influenced by his friends	Makes up his own mind
Does not consider his future	Has clear ambitions and goals and is working towards something even if it changes.
Takes no responsibility for his wrongdoings	Willing to admit his mistakes and to do better.
Indecisive	Able to consider the different perspectives of a situation and makes a decision.

Poor communication and does not attempt to improve it	Able to communicate which means listening and speaking
Treats women with little respect	Understands the value of a woman and speaks/ behaves respectfully
Lies (including withholding truth)	Protects his integrity and is honest no matter the consequences.
Driven by his sexual urges	Demonstrates self-control over his sexual urges
Comfortable with the woman leading	Willing to assume the leadership role of the relationship
Avoids conversations about the relationship. Always wanting to hang in the moment.	Open to conversations about the relationship, has a plan or direction in mind. Open about his intentions

Lazy	Hard-working in whatever capacity. By his sweat, man shall eat bread
Poor relationship with God and no actions to improve intimacy	Has an intimate relationship with God, and this demonstrated by his lifestyle

And so, on....

You may have met a Godly man, but he is NOT ready for a relationship. It would be great if all guys were upfront with this information, but sisters, we need to ask some pertinent questions before we open our hearts. You only have ONE life to live, so invest your most valuable resource (time) well. Of course, it might take some due diligence; or a one on one conversation to find out whether you have happened across a man who is a serious contender for your heart.

A Godly man that is ready

Oh, Lord. I feel like this group of men are an endangered species. I like to call them Unicorns. Hah. Or we can call them a 'MR' meaning marriage ready. They do exist. God will provide. We do not have to side pieces or spinsters.

A MR has the attributes that I listed above for a Godly man. Besides, he is not shady about his movements with you. He verbalises his thoughts about you and what his intentions are upfront. Even if you choose to make, allow him to sweat a little, you do not have to be so available. His pursuit will be relentless. He does not take NO for a final answer even if he gives you some space. On his part, he is consistent. He may also offer to be your friend if you turn him down. And it is for you to decide on what you want to do.

I am just going to list some things that a MR exhibit. He may think he is ready, but you got to confirm that for yourself. It may take some dates, phone calls, research, social media crawling and market research.

Gather the information organically and naturally, avoid making it feel like a job interview. Even though this potential role is way more important than a job interview, you can change jobs as a natural course of life, but marrying the wrong guy can mess up your life.

The GREEN FLAGS

Financially responsible

I did not say rich. Sometimes you have to build the empire together, but one of the most common causes of divorce is finances. Does he make sensible choices with his money? Does he have a way of supporting you? Does he have any addictions or gambling habits? Does he save and invest for the future?

Vision

He has an idea of where he wants you guys to be in a few years. He knows what he wants and is putting the plan in motion. Not just talk, because faith without work is dead. It is alright to be dreamer, but when you wake up, will the thing you dreamt materialise?

Relationship

A man who prioritises spiritual development and worship to God. If he does not lead you to Christ, then he is not the right one. Worship is more than two hours on a Sunday; it is a lifestyle. Does he walk out his faith?

Prioritises

A man who is willing to invest time in developing the relationship. If he is so into his career, he has no time to nurture your relationship. Like a plant, relationships require attention, time and love. It needs a dedicated captain to steer the relation 'ship' in the right direction through the tumultuous waters of life.

Studies

I learnt this from the renown, Pastor Jerry Flowers. The man of God studies you. He wants to learn what makes you tick. He takes notice of the small details and remembers conversations. There is an interest in your future and how he can support you in it.

Servant

I also noted this point down from Jerry Flowers! The man knows how to serve. The place with ample opportunity is in Church. Community outreach and other such programs are even more significant. A hallmark of Christ is humility. Does he display this attribute? Is he loyal? Accountable to leaders? Diligent in his duties? Takes pride in doing the small stuff? This is a big green flag.

Core values

Both of your core values line up. You both want children? You accept foundational principles in the Bible. You have the same understanding of what rape, domestic violence, abuse and infidelity is. You agree on the role of a husband and wife. You kind of know what direction your life is heading or what you both are working towards.

There are so many other things that can be included in this list, but I am just giving up some ideas. I recommend a book called 'Before I do' by Td Jakes. (6)

Conclusion

We have walked through and hopefully out of Mudholes that a single Sister could get her heels stuck into. I could have filled the book with lots more examples, but I feel these are some of the most common things I hear about. Even if you think you are caught in a mudhole right now, you can get out. God has something better in store for you. I appreciate that it may be difficult to walk away from some mudholes. It may be hard, but I encourage you to trust in the Lord with all your heart and lean not unto your own understanding. In all your ways acknowledge Him, and He will direct your path (Proverbs 3:5.) From this day on you will be better at navigating around mudholes. You are on an incredible journey and what is ahead of you is far more exciting than what is behind.

[Hab 3:19 KJV] 19 The LORD God [is] my strength, and he will make my feet like hinds' [feet], and he will make me to walk upon mine high places....

[Psa 32:8 KJV] 8 I will instruct thee and teach thee in the way which thou shalt go: I will guide thee with mine eye.

[Isa 26:7 NLT] 7 But for those who are righteous, the way is not steep and rough. You are a God who does what is right, and you smooth out the path ahead of them.

These three verses bring me such comfort because God will never let you navigate singlehood alone. He has promised in His word to give us wisdom when we ask for it.

Do not be afraid of making mistakes or failing. Things may go wrong even when you try to do everything right. The heart of man can be fickle, and some love connections will catch you off guard. You are human dealing with imperfect humans. However, be comforted that your God will watch out for you.

There were many times I cried because God suddenly broke off a relationship I was trying to form. At the time, it hurt me, but when I looked back, all I can do is thank the Lord. He was protecting me and pulling me out of a mudhole. Do not fight God if He says 'step away' or 'do not go there.' Obedience will save you from tears. Obedience will bring blessings your way.

There is no perfect man, but there are men that are perfect for you. Do not cast your pearls into mudholes because they are destined for your King.

Chapter FIVE

_____Healthy Sexuality_____

I want to hold my hands up. This chapter was not easy for me to write because it destroys the good girl image I have worked so hard to keep up. I am human, and I like people to think well of me. So even though it meant hiding a deep secret that was killing me internally, I did wore a mask for a very long time.

I was that annoying pious girl who was quick to cast judgement on others who had fallen short. Today, I ask for forgiveness from anyone and everyone I have needlessly offended. At times, I was loudly projecting the condemnation I was quietly serving myself. I knew right from wrong, I had scriptures for days, but still, I was struggling with my sexual integrity. This is the metaphorical room in the house of my life that was in disarray for a very long time.

I know I am not the only one.

Some blessed women among us walk around unbothered by the lack of sex in their lives. Some of these women may be asexual, and the others have low libido. I am in neither one of these groups.

At 11 years old, I stumbled upon pornography in literature form. I was a book worm, and I wormed my way through all the children books. There were hundreds of titles assessable to me, but I was precocious. One day, I remember nothing unusual about it, but I was drawn to a contemporary novel written about black culture.

I enjoyed this particular romance novel because the characters were black, and they spoke like the Americans on the TV. I recognise that I have been a 'hopeless romantic' from a very early age. The storyline had me, next thing I know I was like WHOA.... HE DID WHAT? HE TOUCHED HER WHERE?

The writer was inept at explaining how the leading lady felt, and it immediately drew me in. Boom! Just like that, something woke up in me. Faster than a click of the fingers, I entered puberty. I was not abused; my parents were very vigilant about what TV I was exposed to and where I went. I knew it was a grown-up book when I encountered profanity, but I was also precocious. I found it off my own back. The kids spoke about naughty things at school, though I was not interested in it until that moment. I did not go looking for porn, yet porn found me.

The Internet thing was just becoming popular and accessible. So once I was hooked I was soon able to log on and read fan fiction sites for B2K, which was just as graphic as the novel. That same year I was introduced to sex education at school. I cannot remember the order of events; only at some point, I realised that my vajay was for more than passing urine. That "making love" was something that grown-ups did, and it felt good. Unknowingly I had entered a battle that even today, I still fight to be perfectly honest. At

11, I knew this new habit I was forming was wrong. I kept it secret, I repented, but I also kept going back. Each time I said sorry Jesus I genuinely believed it was the last time.

The initial pay off was a physical high that only lasted minutes, but after that, the guilt and self-loathing set in. I got used to making up fantasies. I was the person in the story. I pretended. I found out that the boys were not interested in fat girls, so I felt rejected as a girl growing up. But in my fantasies, I was desirable; my body was not repulsive but made me feel good. It was my secret shame, and even though I hid this habit in the dark corners of my life, the consequences became visible.

Over the years, I began to access photo and video pornography. I cannot remember the exact date. But I do remember entering a Google search for sex-related words and seeing what came up. I used to cry because I felt so guilty and that God was not going to love me anymore. The material I needed became more and more explicit. I did not know at the time that lust had an appetite that could not be satisfied and had no absolute limits. It was never enough. I trusted no one with my secret war.

Masturbation is a very private affair... says she who is sharing her testimony. It is an activity that usually does not directly involve another person. I learnt how to make excuses to God: "It is not as bad, I cannot get pregnant, I am not having sex. If you did not want me to do it, then it would be impossible, like tickling myself or licking my elbows." I thought I could just compartmentalise that part of my life. Lock that room in the house of my life and live happily in the remaining places.

At my best, I went for months not doing anything, but something inevitably would trigger me off. When I was in despair, or I needed a pick me up. I may have seen something in that movie turned me on, but I needed to turn off. Romance in any media form triggered me. And it was hard to break the relapse routine. My logic went something like this: "I am already in trouble for taking this lipstick might as well take a pack of crisps and this lilt, well fine, grabbing that chocolate is not going to make a difference." Presumptuous and repetitive sin is like having a dead body under the floorboards, the stench seeps out and desecrates the whole building. This was not an ordinary sin; this was a lifestyle and mental stronghold that was not quickly broken.

God's love was consistent, but there were constant uneasiness and tension to our relationship. I was not at peace or comfortable; so far away from living the abundant life, Christ died to give me. I thought I could handle it on my own, but I flat out refused to surrender my body to God. I felt this was all I had to make me feel like a real woman.

I already suffered from very low self-esteem, so this secret battle just stomped me down another two feet. I overcompensated in other areas to try and offset my spiritual rebellion. I "went in" (British street slang for excelled, put maximal effort) one hundred and ten per cent with my education. I ran for church member of the year (not real), holding down lots of positions from worship leader to dance coordinator to youth worker. Throughout this period, God still spoke to me. He even used me to minister because spiritual gifts are given without repentance. This is precisely what Jesus was talking about in Matthew in His sermon on the mount. There will be many on judgement day saying "Lord did I not do this in your name? Look how many people got saved under my ministry? I sang gospel and blessed thousands of people. You healed people through me." And sadly, God will say: "depart from me, I know you not."

I know all about the double life. You are one way in church and around Christian friends, but behind closed doors, it is another story. It is a dire situation to find yourself in. Just remember, that even if God uses you, it does not mean He approves you. If I had been cut off suddenly from the land of the living back then, there was a significant chance that I would have gone to hell. I am saved only because of God's mercy.

I remember gorging on so much literary porn that I could write my own. If I did, the story would have easily knocked out fifty shades of foolishness. Well, this was in the days of Myspace and MSN. Whatever you feed grows stronger right? So I built a monster-sized spiritual giant pretty quickly. As I exposed myself to more and more explicit material, I opened the door for the enemy to have legal access to influence over my life.

The Devil will stop at nothing to destroy your relationship with God and decimate your destiny. Do not underestimate this opponent. I know the enemy studies you and will tempt you with a vice attractive to you. I found evidence to support in James where it talks about being enticed by own lusts. And here is the kicker, the Devil will not wait until you are grown to attack, he will seize the first opportunity he gets when you are young.

I feel that in many Christian homes, the conversation about sex occurs far too late if it occurs at all. When I went to primary school, they started educating us about sex at 10 or 11, but now I am sure it is earlier 5/6. This is during our formative years, where the child is most susceptible to indoctrination. When you allow secular institutions to educate children on morality and identity, that is precisely what is going on here indoctrination to demonic agendas. Children are exposed to sexual content from a very young age. It is in advertising, the dance moves they imitate, the songs they sing, pop videos that are playing in the salons while mums get their nails done, and celebrities who they look up to often are not age or faith appropriate.

If a parent is reading this, I appreciate that sex is such a delicate matter. I share your concern about over-exposure and ruining childhood innocence. You do want to protect your child from anything that would harm their peace and development. So the maturity of the child and their ability to understand the information should be considered. Always ask the Holy Spirit for wisdom to know when what and how to broach the subject. Just do not let the school system get in there first, and it is not always in the curriculum. It is the other children in school your child interacts with. When they are exposed to something, they share it. I would encourage you to oversee the learning process about sex. Informing your child is not going to expedite experimentation or sexual activity. What it will do is open up a dialogue for questions. It will provide an opportunity to teach what to do before their hormones start raging. They need to make sense of the sex-saturated world that they live in and be clear about how born again Christians differ in their morals and lifestyle.

When I got to 15, all hell broke loose. I was into the whole MSN meeting guys online thing. And let us just say my imagination and writing skills came into good use. I was popular online; I catfished mostly because some of these guys I knew I would never meet in real life. I had fun. I was a Netflix series, a straight 'A' student, an active member of the church and behaving like a 'lady of the night' online. In this virtual world, I was desired, fussed over, I was important, I was attractive. I did not feel that in real life. I never had a boyfriend, no one liked me, and all crushes had rejected me to my face. I kind of went a bit silly in the head and started meeting these guys in real life. At one point, at my worst, I was talking to about 12 guys at the same time. We had zero in common apart from the fact that we were horny teenagers. Mad.

What were my parents doing??? Remember I was a Bishops daughter? I was raised in a Christian home and taught right from wrong. Well, they were fire fighting. I got my computer confiscated, wires taken, phones taken. I shouted, slammed doors, cried myself to sleep, I lied to them, I ate so much food I would feel physically sick, I harmed myself a couple of times. I tried to jump out a window twice, and I was the most volatile child around at times.

I know that I was a handful to raise, and my parents did an excellent job to support me through this nightmare. I told them very little about what I was facing because I did not want to disappoint them.

When a teenager is acting out, you often see the fruit of the problem, and it is a mammoth job to find the root. If they are anything like me and do not want to let you in... they will not. My parent knew that I was sad, and I had some complicated issues, but they could not fix it themselves.

The prayers of a righteous man/woman are very effective, and God did step in. I almost hated them at times, oh yes, but it is only now as a grown woman I can appreciate the length they went to, to help me, support me and love me. It was their unconditional love that kept me in the land of the living. So as tempting as it is to point fingers at my parents, it boiled down to my decision, and I was determined to do whatever I wanted. I figured I had tried things God's way, and he was not going to give me a boyfriend. So I would take control of my love life.

One of my triggers for pornography was stress. Stress is something you cannot avoid. It was a complex and destructive cycle because I had poor coping strategies.:

[Figure 2: The Sin Self Harm Cycle]

I thought I had defeated this sexual sin cycle several times. I had prayed, fasted, rolled around at the altar at a fiery convention many times. This is it! This is the last time! I thought I had evicted those demons from my life, yet I left the doors and windows open. I was in denial. It is NOT just a river in Egypt. BADOOM CHA! I just wanted to lighten the mood. Smile nuh? :) It gets better.

God and I have been on a journey. Nothing can make me leave my God because He has always been there for me. I thought I had exhausted His grace and patience. I had given up on myself, but God has NEVER given up on me. He is a good Father... that is who He is.

I say this with confidence: You may be facing your battles, maybe you like having sex, and you do not know how you are going to stop. You know it is not right, but you are tired of the shame cycle. God is not shocked, or surprised, He has seen everything, and He still loves you. Christ can set you free permanently!

We talked about stress as being an unavoidable trigger, but there are other... like hormones. At a specific time of the month, I felt I needed a physical high. My hormones were raging, and what could I do about it? I did not have to watch anything or talk to anybody to get going. It was as if I was physically programmed to experience a craving for sex in time with my egg release.

I read some research on the topic, and basically, women are complex. There is so much variability in each women's libido, the number of hormones they secrete and length of the menstruation cycle. So far, scientists have yet to come up with an answer to determine which hormones cause sexual arousal and when it is most likely to happen. Woman... just know thyself lol!

Masturbation and Pornography

Very few people masturbate for enjoyment; it is not the preferred sexual activity. People masturbate because of habit/addiction, because of their sex drive and a lack of another outlet for sex.

Masturbation is a big deal. I know there is no scripture instructing us on masturbation word for Word, but there are plenty scriptures about sexual purity and self-control. The Bible says that you can do all things, but not all things are beneficial. So you physically can scratch a sexual itch, but it does not help you in the long run.

You have first to accept that what you do in the flesh has an impact on your spirit. I was reading Romans 8 recently, and it talks about following after the flesh and the way it leads to destruction. The way I understand it is our body. It is not saved. It is the house of your soul and spirit. It's only desire is to please itself. Your flesh is what connects you to this earth world, and it is all about what you can sense: touch, taste, smell, see and hear. Your flesh represents your carnal mind, the one you had before you accepted Jesus as your Lord and personal Saviour. That is why every believer needs to go through sanctification after salvation. There has to be a renewal of the mind to accommodate the will of God. Your natural tendency is to do things that feel good to your body, but are sinful and damaging to your spirit. It is God who awakens that desire in us to please Him and empowers us to do so.

Again I will acknowledge that people get caught up on the fact there is no specific verse in the Bible that says: Thou shall not touch yourself to the point of orgasm. God does not have to put a particular verse in if you understand the verse about no sexual immorality. There comes the point in your walk with God when you stop looking for loopholes and defaults. Your love for Him fuels your desire to learn Him. Once you understand the Heart of Father and that the Word in its in entirety,

He answers every question. There is no confusion regarding masturbation/pornography only rejection of His authority over your life.

The Bible also never mentioned cybersex, phone sex, erotic novels, steamy movies, TV shows or rampant rabbits... You know the heart of your Father is for you to be holy and to worship Him with your lifestyle. It is for you to present your body to Him as a living sacrifice. His will is that you learn how to possess your flesh as a vessel of honour. That you will not have sex with yourself because it involves sexualised thoughts. It creates a doorway of influence from the Enemy.

Remember, Satan's job is to get in the way of your relationship with God. The last thing you want to do after masturbating is to talk to God. You start to pull your heart away from God, and that distance can turn into long term separation.

Masturbation is short term gain with long term loss; then you throw in adverse side effects. It will never be enough. We were not meant to have solo sex as a replacement or temporary fix before marriage. If masturbation was able to satisfy the soul and the longing for intimacy; why would Paul say it was better to marry than to burn? Surely if masturbation were enough, then it would extinguish the flames? (Corinthians 7:7-9)

We, women, have vivid imaginations, and in theory, if it was the plan of God for you to be your lover, then masturbation should completely eradicate the desire for physical intimacy. However, we all know sex is not just about the climax. It is more than the 5-second orgasm. It is the journey to the peak. During the journey, there are emotional and psychological needs being met. There is a need for validation, affirmation, appreciation and acceptance. The most physical representation of marriage (sex) meets these needs. It is supposed to bond you with your husband. There is spiritual activity going on that cannot even be easily explained in the natural.

I have looked at this issue from the top, bottom, side, diagonal, near, far, read, fasted, meditated, pondered. And my conclusion after 15 years is that....

Masturbation does not satisfy your needs.

Masturbation works against your peace; it wedges shame into your relationship with God. You hide like Adam and Eve after they ate the fruit. It also creates unrealistic expectations for your future husband. Forget your future husband, sex now in your mind becomes wholly centred on yourself. It is no longer an expression of love between man and wife. It teaches you that your 'needs' are more significant than God's will. It shows you that the flesh cannot be denied. It fills your mind with ungodly thoughts. It feeds lust, and we know that monster can never be satisfied. Lust will have you doing some crazy things with crazy consequences.

Masturbation is an addictive temporary distraction that feeds lust and makes you more likely to compromise your sexual purity later on. It is a mind thing and self-control thing. In Proverbs, it says a person without self-control is like a city without walls. Masturbation leaves you vulnerable to attack by the Enemy. It is harder to maintain sexual integrity when you regularly engage in masturbation because you know what you want. It is like you have experienced a diluted version of sex, and there will be a stronger desire for the real thing.

It is tough if not impossible, to stimulate yourself without any sexual thought. If you can, I guess you are similar to a sex robot. Usually, you have to fantasise about a scenario where you are observing sexual activity or participating in it. This spirals out of control faster then you can say: "but I am a Christian!" You will find that you need more and more sexually explicit stimuli to get you over the hill. And when it is done, it satisfies the flesh but torments the spirit.

I have experienced an emotional hangover. I do not drink to get drunk, so I have not experienced a real hangover. But I have had a headache, nausea, fatigue and tired head after porn binge. After those few seconds/minutes of physical pleasure that masturbation can bring, almost immediately, there is an emotional hangover. It is as if you have stepped into a trap, triggered it and now you are hanging in a net not sure of how you are going to get down.

I think the same thing happens to born again Christian singles who engage in premarital sexual activity. Some of you reading are in sexual relationships right now. You say it is complicated because you love him. You may also say it is not a big deal. But we both know it is. The spirit is always in contention with the flesh, and if the flesh wins... it affects you. You feel guilty and disappointed that you were weak again and caved in.

If you have not become desensitised to the Holy Spirit, He convicts you. You feel Godly sorrow, which is good because it shows your heart is still yearning for God. When you do not feel any remorse or concern... that is a bigger problem. I call it being spiritually dead, that relationship connection with God has been severed. Jesus came to earth to reconnect you, so if you find yourself in this place, far from Father, there is life, it is not too late.

The Holy Spirit personally guides you in all truth, and that is how I knew that masturbation was wrong. I read the publications from perverted Christian authors and so-called experts encouraging people to do it. They had all kinds of reasons, scientific papers and psychologist statements to back it up. I remember reading a website saying: think about Jesus and give Him praise while you are enjoying yourself at this moment! And it is safety pressure valve, masturbate before you go on a date and you are less likely to have sex. That is garbage!

PORN STORY

Sex in the right context of heterosexual marriage as defined by God is amazing (so I hear). I cannot stand the super conservative Christians who pretend all 15 of their children just appeared one day. Sex is a beautiful gift from God. What Satan does, because he cannot create, is to corrupt. He corrupts the conditions God gave to govern sex. He promotes the exact conceptual opposite of what God wants. Sex is no longer privately exclusive to the heterosexual married couple.

Born again Christians who believe the Bible has authority, tend to accept pornography is wrong without much argument. (There are still some who flat out reject the truth.... We will continue to pray) In Matthew 5:28, Jesus makes it abundantly clear that lust is a sin. If seeing something triggers a sexual thought about a person who is not your spouse, God views those thoughts as sinful. It is considered as immoral as the act itself. You may not act it out physically, but you have rebelled against the rules governing sex in your heart.

The idea behind porn is, whether you realise or not, you are participating in the sexual act you are watching/reading. You do not physically have to be present to be involved. Exchanging sex emails, sext messages, talking about sexual acts on the phone are all variations of the same thing. All these things feed your mind material to stimulate a sexual response in your body to someone you are not married to. You can be sexually active, even if you have not physically touched anyone.

As this is a book written for single Christian women, even if you are in dating/courting relationship... your significant other is NOT your husband yet.

It is one thing to watch a TV commercial where a couple suddenly starts making out; you may be turned on by those steamy scenes unintentionally. It is an entirely different matter to keep rewinding that segment because you want to continue being sexually excited.

More often than not, you will not be physically satisfied until you climax.

For some, porn does not have to be hardcore and graphic. Merely looking at a poster of a half naked celebrity is enough to create sexual fantasies. When I talk about sexual purity, I do not think it is helpful to describe rules and literal lines that should not be crossed, because everyone is different. Everyone has different preferences and tolerance levels.

God did not list out every single scenario explicitly; so I try to apply biblical principles in a mature manner that comes from understanding the heart of the Father. The Holy Spirit helped me to think of porn as any form of media that is sexual in nature, that turns me on outside of my future husband. Sounds extreme, but as a principle it works for me by leaving no room for lust in my life.

There are spiritual aspects to porn because we are spirits who dwell in a human body. Assessing sexual material outside of your spouse is an act of disobedience to God. It can open your life up to spiritual attacks from the enemy. It even changes the spiritual atmosphere of where you are. Light and darkness do not co-exist, and it is left to us to make a choice. As a child of God, you are at war, and sin can disarm you, leaving you vulnerable. You have free will to step outside the covering of God. It is up to His grace and mercy to rescue you, never take it for granted... I tested God's patience, trust me; this is I know He is God.

Porn is designed to indulge your flesh. Whatever your carnal desires are, you are encouraged to pursue them. It is in direct conflict to our promise to God, which is to present ourselves to Him as a living sacrifice. Porn destroys your sexual innocence which in turn perverts your sexual preferences. It aims to please the carnal unsaved flesh at whatever cost. The explicit images cannot be easily erased so that the enemy will flick on that movie screen at the weirdest of times. It influences the way you see people, without really wanting to.

Porn taught me how to be sexy according to its standards (which is unrealistic.) If I got into a situation with a guy, lust kicked in, and I would go on automatic pilot. My body would know what to do, and I felt I knew what I wanted. To give up my dream of being a virgin when I get married was too easy when I was not even thinking deeply about what I was doing. You just lived in the moment. And what you are doing more often than not feels good at the time.

What starts as an innocent exploration can turn into risky experimentation. It amazes me how fast the material you get through can escalate because you become desensitised very quickly. Much like other drugs, you need more and more to get the same high as you did before. You start looking for more material, more explicit, more perverse. LUST HAS NO GENDER

PREFERENCE. The spirit of lust does not appear to have any rules.

Pornography should be taken seriously; it does not just adversely affect Christians. Over the years, I have read articles and studies that highlight how easily those addicted to porn can find themselves seeking illicit material. The spirit of lust can be so strong and influential; as its ultimate aim to is desecrate life. Studies claim that those identified as sexually deviant in society tend to have pornography addictions. Including and not limited to those who engage in incest, rape, bestiality, paedophilia and masochism (I know masochism is not illegal), it is a multibillion-pound industry. So we cannot expect the dangers to be well publicised. (7)

Porn was created to enslave you to a fantasy world. Giving pleasure to your flesh but poisoning your spirit, it subconsciously creates an unrealistic expectation of what sex will be like. Although in saying that, there has been a gigantic boom in-home/amateur videos. People want to be famous and sell themselves. This, I think, is in direct correlation with the social media boom. People are a lot more willing to share private details of their life. This graphic exploitation of what is supposed to be a sacred covenant violates your future sex life with your husband. The marriage bed God says is undefiled; nevertheless, porn is one of the ways to defile it.

I do not know how to dress it up or look at it from another perspective. From every angle, it is a sin (sin = misses the mark or expectation that God has for humankind). It tries to divorce emotional commitment from the physical act of having an orgasm. There is a spiritual aspect. It kills the fruit of the spirit and replaces it with works of the flesh. It strips you of your holiness, making it very difficult to connect to God. That isolation tactic is lethal. You feel safe on your side of the screen, but your spirit is crying inside.

I will repeat this! Many are hung up on the fact the word porn is not used in the Bible. A mature Christian seeks to understand the heart of God. You are not looking for loopholes to get away with doing your own thing. You also have to use your logic of understanding the text, and the Holy Spirit gives revelation. (I know the English version we have is not the original text, but you know what I mean) If the Bible says do not kill... you cannot come back and say; "Can I strangle someone? The Bible did not say not to strangle. What about poisoning someone? I do not see the word poison." You know that these are just classifications of the same thing. They are all forms of killing someone—same thing for porn. God said to abstain from sexual immorality. This means EVERY form of sexual immorality. Whether it is engaging in threesomes, watching sex on TV, homosexuality or sex with the boyfriend. He warned us that these acts are sinful. (1 Cor 6:9)

I did not want to bore you with a long, drawn-out history of pornography. Humans have been expressing their sexual thoughts in art form since prehistoric times. I am serious; Wikipedia said they had found explicit doodles in caves from the stone-age. Modern-day Western culture appears to be significantly influenced by Roman/Greek philosophy. This hedonistic, sexual liberation, the hippie movement was suppressed during specific periods of history; but has re-emerged to dominate our world today. Porn now comes in so many different forms due to technological advancements and social morality shifts. Sexual promiscuity and hedonism are again at the height of society, so it is widely accepted, but God's will for His people remains the same.

Scriptures for dealing with sexual sin

The Holy Spirit is a fantastic person who guides us in all truth. I found these following scriptures very useful in helping me identify porn as a sinful stronghold and helped me break it.

I feel the need to reiterate that your love for God is your basis for reading the Bible. Those who do not love God will not fully understand it and therefore, will not be willing to accept its teaching. It is a vast library of 66 books written over hundreds of years by dozens of men. I believe it was written under the divine inspiration of the Holy Spirit. I take it seriously; I think it fits together perfectly. I think some concepts are better understood with maturity, so you must incorporate Bible study as a core discipline for personal development.

The Bible is God's expressed Word that reveals His nature, our identity, the reality we live in and His will for mankind. The Holy Spirit has been charged with the responsibility to teach us and guide us in all truth. He helps us apply the Word to everyday life. It is not supposed to be a chore, and it is supposed to be food for your soul. It cleanses your thought life and thus strengthens your faith. You cannot expect to be a strong Christian without knowing God's Word for yourself; it is essential like oxygen to the physical body.

On the 'Youversion' Bible app, there is a devotional series that gives terrific advice in the introduction of the daily scripture. Seek to turn an empty religious act of reading the Bible like a shampoo ingredients list, into a valuable activity that will enhance your spiritual life.

They suggest prayer first to focus your mind on God. To create an environment where you can hear what the Holy Spirit has to say. Please read the text, read it in a translation you understand. There is so many version available which each have different purposes. I would say always compare versions to ensure you do not miss out on details of the scripture. Of course, the original language is Hebrew. The Message Bible, I think, is excellent for understanding the emotion and tone of a verse. I learn from the Amplified Version and memorise King James simply because I like the way it sounds.

I am going to annotate and exegete these texts to share my understanding, I am sorry if it seems a lot, but these are words of life. There is no rush to work your way through. I pray that God will speak to your heart.

Matthew 5:27-28

"You have heard that it was said, 'YOU SHALL NOT COMMIT ADULTERY'; but I say to you that everyone who looks at a woman with lust for her has already committed adultery with her in his heart.

Here I believe Jesus is taking the laws that were given to Moses and showing us how to fulfil it more thoroughly. We know that Christ fulfilled the righteous component of the law for us. In exchange, He expects to walk in holiness. The heart of the Father is that we are holy as He is holy. Therefore we have a responsibility to understand His commandments and apply them with the help of the Holy Spirit.

Looking with sinful intent is just as bad as acting the sin out. God sees it as the same because He looks at the heart. When we put things before our eyes that are not conducive to our spiritual growth, it influences our thoughts. And thoughts become the motivation for our actions. This is why I say.... Nothing happens. The expression of sin begins with the idea in your heart.

Without trying to be deep, this scripture is relevant to pornography. When you watch sexual content for stimulation, you are lusting for that person and participating in that activity. Adultery encompasses fornication, sexual activity outside of a marital union. God confirmed in so many places Old Testament and New Testament that He takes sexual sin seriously.

Romans 12:1-9

I appeal to you therefore, brothers, by the mercies of God, to present your bodies as a living sacrifice, holy and acceptable to God, which is your spiritual worship. Do not be conformed to this world, but be transformed by the renewal of your mind, that by testing you may discern what is the will of God, what is good and acceptable and perfect....

The only way we can live transformed lives is to allow God to renew the way we think. Presenting our bodies to God as a living sacrifice means doing things that please Him, not ourselves. Porn is about wanting yourself at the expense of your purity. It takes a conscious decision to present yourself to God every day. This is one of my favourite scriptures, which emphasises that what you think determines your actions and the success of your life.

Matthew 6:22-23

"The eye is the lamp of the body. So, if your eye is healthy, your whole body will be full of light, but if your eye is bad, your whole body will be full of darkness. If then the light in you is darkness, how great is the darkness!

There is no way you can have a pure thought life if you feed your mind with rubbish. This scripture emphasises the importance of moderating what I watch, listen to, participate in. No one has to tell me or set rules for me because the Holy Spirit and I are in partnership. I do not want to be overcome by the desires of my flesh, so I have to be proactive in guarding my thoughts. Whatever you feed will be strengthened. So one of the ways my sexual integrity is maintained is that my media diet is healthy.

On a deeper level, your 'eye' can represent your understanding, perspective and approach to life. When your 'eye' is pure, it means your entire life is pure and full of revelation. When you are ignorant of the things of God, then your life is whole of confusion.

Psalm 101:3

I will not set before my eyes anything that is worthless...

This is self explanatory. Use it in your prayer times and morning/evening declarations.

1 Corinthians 6:18-20

Flee immorality. Every other sin that a man commits is outside the body, but the immoral man sins against his own body. Or do you not know that your body is a temple of the Holy Spirit who is in you, whom you have from God, and that you are not your own? For you have been bought with a price: therefore glorify God in your body.

I like this scripture because it showed me that sometimes God does not even want me to get into the boxing ring with sin. There is a temptation to overestimate how much we can handle. God is saying here, very simply, run away from the very appearance of evil. Do not even go to examine it and see if you can stand up to it. RUN.

We are supposed to be carriers of the very Spirit and presence of God. We cannot desecrate our temples and expect God to chill in us as nothing happened. It offends Him and does negatively affect our relationship. I saw in this scripture the value that God places on all aspects of life. Yes, my body eventually will return to dust, but I have to give an account for what I do in this temporary temple. I am charged with the responsibility to glorify God with how I take care of this gift. The Blood of Jesus redeemed me, and you were too.

1 Corinthians 6:13

"Food is meant for the stomach and the stomach for food"—and God will destroy both one and the other.

The body is not meant for sexual immorality, but for the Lord, and the Lord for the body.

Self explanatory again. The priority for us on earth is not to live to please ourselves but the one who created us.

Ephesians 5:11-12

Do not participate in the unfruitful deeds of darkness, but instead even expose them; for it is disgraceful even to speak of the things, which are done by them in secret.

Watching pornography is participation in deeds of darkness. The reason companies and pornstars made the video was to engage an audience. To entertain, stimulate responses and influence your behaviour. There are other things tend to be done in private like 'overeating,' 'self-harming,' or 'negative talking.' These secret things cause stress, and they can harm your health. Often the habits create a barrier between yourself and God.

There is a natural reaction to run from His presence when we sin. But the instruction is to expose deeds of darkness. God is not scared of dealing with your problems and issues. Allow God to step into your situation. He can turn things around. He will connect you with people that will help you. Jesus died to ensure your freedom from destructive addictions.

1 Thessalonians 5:22

...abstain from every form of evil.

Do not participate, involve yourself, observe, entangle, touch, handle, or attach yourself to evil things.

1 John 3:4-10

Everyone who makes a practice of sinning also practices lawlessness; sin is lawlessness. You know that he (Jesus) appeared to take away sins, and in him there is no sin. No one who abides in him keeps on sinning; no one who keeps on sinning has either seen him or known him. Little children, let no one deceive you. Whoever practices righteousness is righteous, as he is righteous. Whoever makes a practice of sinning is of the devil, for the devil has been sinning from the beginning. The reason the Son of God appeared was to destroy the works of the devil.

If you continue to sin, you cannot say that you know God. Your actions have to match up to your profession of faith. There is no room for presumptuous sin where you feel God does not mind sinful habits. He does mind. Your sinful habits cost Jesus His life. Jesus died to set you free, so you cannot keep on sinning. When you continue in sin, you are rejecting the freedom He has offered to remain in bondage. You are what you do. And what you do comes from what you think.

John 14:15

"If you love me, you will keep my commandments

Another no-nonsense scripture. Either you love God, or you do not. This rechallenged my attitude on presumptuous sin. The Devil wanted me to feel comfortable with the idea that I can do whatever I want, say I am sorry, and everything would be alright.

There were times I thought that the habit could never be kicked, only managed in terms of frequency.

The Word that was in me was at war with the world around me. I was at conflict with myself because I knew who I wanted to serve, God; but I was practising things that did not please Him. I made the mistake of thinking for years I could get myself out of it. I just needed to trust in the last part of the verse, which depended on the Son of God to destroy the works of the Devil.

1 Thessalonians 4:3-6

For this is the will of God, your sanctification: that you abstain from sexual immorality; that each one of you know how to control his own body in holiness and honor, not in the passion of lust like the Gentiles who do not know God; that no one transgress and wrong his brother in this matter, because the Lord is an avenger in all these things, as we told you beforehand and solemnly warned you.

This is precisely what this book is about... learning how to control your body in holiness and honour. I am comforted that it is a process of unlearning and mind renewal in the Word. For those who are having sex...

there it is. It is God's will that you remain set apart from sin. He wants you to refrain from using sex outside its holy parameters which is marriage.

James 1:14-15

But each one is tempted when he is carried away and enticed by his own lust. Then when lust has conceived, it gives birth to sin; and when sin is accomplished, it brings forth death.

I thought this scripture was interesting because it highlighted how different things would tempt different people. I believe the Devil can custom make set up scenarios to grab your attention. Here we can see evidence for the consequential chain reaction that I mentioned before. Death can be in its natural form, but I also interpret it to be separated from God. You can be alive but separated from God by being spiritually dead.

1 Peter 2:11

Beloved, I urge you as sojourners and exiles to abstain from the passions of the flesh, which wage war against your soul.

This scripture is so special to me because it reminds me that my life is not just restricted to earth. I am simply a pilgrim passing through. One day my weak flesh corrupted by sin will be exchanged for a great upgrade. I will live in the presence of God for all eternity. And so what I do down here, matters and my purity is worth fighting for. I am locked into a war, but that through Christ... I have already won. I am tearing up thinking about the journey, but God is so good and faithful.

Ephesians 2:3

Among whom we all once lived in the passions of our flesh, carrying out the desires of the body and the mind, and were by nature children of wrath, like the rest of mankind.

I accepted Christ as my Lord and personal Saviour and was reborn spiritually into the Kingdom of God. I am no longer a child of wrath. I have access to the power and strength that others do not. I am not living to serve my flesh but living for a better purpose. I am not a slave to sin. I have freedom in Christ.

2 Corinthians 10:4-6

For the weapons of our warfare are not of the flesh but have divine power to destroy strongholds. We destroy arguments and every lofty opinion raised against the knowledge of God, and take every thought captive to obey Christ, being ready to punish every disobedience, when your obedience is complete.

This one of my favourite battle scriptures and I use it often in prayer to remind myself of the position of power I am praying from. My thoughts must be brought into subjection and alignment with the Will of God. I do not want to be entertaining things that are harmful to my soul. I have weapons of warfare that God puts His power behind that makes an impact on strongholds. When I pray, God sends strength and even fights for me. When I worship, I change the atmosphere of wherever I am, drawing the manifest presence of God closer. Trust me. Your flesh calms down real quick when God shows up tangibly.

Hebrews 12:1

Therefore, since we are surrounded by so great a cloud of witnesses, let us also lay aside every weight, and sin which clings so closely, and let us run with endurance the race that is set before us

---

Another favourite. God knows our struggles and areas of difficulty, and He still knows we can win our race. It is a decision of ours to lay aside the things that are dragging us down. It helps me think of myself as an athlete. I have to train intentionally to improve my stamina. I have to adopt the winner's mindset that I can finish strong. There are lifestyle changes I have to make to endure. I love the comparison, and it helped me with my weight loss too. Lay aside EVERY weight, every additional pound of obesity I rebuke in Jesus name lol.

2 Timothy 2:22

So flee youthful passions and pursue righteousness, faith, love, and peace, along with those who call on the Lord from a pure heart.

I interpret this as a matter of spiritual maturity, not just physical age. Whatever age you accept Christ as Saviour, following salvation, you must go through sanctification. There is a growth process that will lead to maturity. Your focus, weaknesses and passions will change as you grow.

I love the fact that the scripture says to pursue the virtues mentioned above.

There is an intentional push... you have to act... you have to make time... you must seek God. Holy Spirit oversees your maturation, but it is a partnership. God ministers to you but the scripture also alludes to the community. The scripture says 'along with those who call on the Lord from a pure heart.' You are not alone in this journey. We are a part of a community. You are not alone in this process, stay connected to people who will support you.

Titus 2:11-14

For the grace of God has appeared, bringing salvation for all people, training us to renounce ungodliness and worldly passions, and to live self-controlled, upright, and godly lives in the present age, waiting for our blessed hope, the appearing of the glory of our great God and Savior Jesus Christ, who gave himself for us to redeem us from all lawlessness and to purify for himself a people for his own possession who are zealous for good works.

I do not need to add anything more. It is beautiful in its simplicity.

Romans 8:1-39

There is therefore now no condemnation for those who are in Christ Jesus. For the law of the Spirit of life has set you free in Christ Jesus from the law of sin and death. For God has done what the law, weakened by the flesh, could not do. By sending his own Son in the likeness of sinful flesh and for sin, he condemned sin in the flesh, in order that the righteous requirement of the law might be fulfilled in us, who walk not according to the flesh but according to the Spirit. For those who live according to the flesh set their minds on the things of the flesh, but those who live according to the Spirit set their minds on the things of the Spirit.

This is the secret; this is chemical X; this is the game-changer. I learnt the long way that you cannot defeat sin in your strength. You have to seek deliverance in Jesus. No amount of positive thinking that is not based on the Word of God will conquer lust. The Bible says the spirit is willing, but the flesh is weak. Breaking. The shame and guilt break the cycle.

I first believe I am forgiven because Jesus took the punishment of my sin for me. I am no longer without hope; I do not have to condemn myself continually. Jesus breaks the power sin has over me. It is like Jesus opening the door of a prison, and my job is to walk through the open door. Once I walk through the open door, to stay free, I keep in step with the Holy Spirit. I do not do the same things I used to because those things lead to bondage. I walk after the Spirit of God, doing as He says. My mind is focused on things that please God. Porn has no place in my life.

Galatians 5:19

Now the works of the flesh are evident: sexual immorality, impurity, sensuality.

Porn is a work of the flesh, the carnal or anti God side.

Romans 6:11-14

So you also must consider yourselves dead to sin and alive to God in Christ Jesus. Let not sin therefore reign in your mortal body, to make you obey its passions. Do not present your members to sin as instruments for unrighteousness, but present yourselves to God as those who have been brought from death to life, and your members to God as instruments for righteousness. For sin will have no dominion over you, since you are not under law but under grace.

Another authoritative scripture that supports what I have just spoken about. In Jesus Christ, I am dead to sin but alive to righteousness, presenting my body to God. It is a good practice to find two or three examples of an idea before you accept it as a precept of God. In the mouths of two or three witnesses let everything be established. God likes to confirm Himself to make sure His will is clear. Peculiar sects and cults that draws from Christianity, often focus on one scripture which without the full context can be misinterpreted and misused to support a bizarre idea they promote. It is commonly used to enforce control. People can be deceived because they do not know the Word of God for themselves. As you study the Word, underline and make a note of scriptures that directly repeat or link to each other.

Galatians 5:13-25

For you were called to freedom, brothers. Only do not use your freedom as an opportunity for the flesh, but through love serve one another. For the whole law is fulfilled in one word: "You shall love your neighbor as yourself." .... But I say, walk by the Spirit, and you will not gratify the desires of the flesh. For the desires of the flesh are against the Spirit, and the desires of the Spirit are against the flesh, for these are opposed to each other, to keep you from doing the things you want to do...

The Bible says to love your neighbour. Who is your neighbour? Everyone that is not yourself. The Bible says to love your enemies. There is no one on planet earth that we should not love. Love does not abuse people or use them for selfish reasons. When you engage in visual pornography, you are using someone to achieve a sexual high. This is not loving. The fact that they may have wilfully put themselves in that position is irrelevant. Do not dehumanise them; they are worthy of respect and love because they are children of God.

This is why God puts His kind of love in our hearts because the unconditional aspect to it is hard to provide. Pornography is renown for causing men and women to view each other as a bunch of body parts. We are more than that. Those people on the screen are someone's daughter or son who has lost their way. Out of love, we have to give them the respect they lack for themselves. Some may feel they are trapped in this world. This attitude of compassionate can help change the way you view pornography.

Proverbs 28:13

Whoever conceals his transgressions will not prosper, but he who confesses and forsakes them will obtain mercy.

I love this proverb. Confession is good for the soul. 1 John 1:9 If we confess our sins, then God is faithful and just and will forgive our sins and purify us from all unrighteousness. God knows everything, but He wants to hear our own words. There has to be an acknowledgement about an issue before you can change it.

This brief list does not include every single scripture that can be directly related to sexual sin, but it is a start. Feel free to copy them out and write down your thoughts on what God is saying to you. Use them to form prayers about the subject. Praying the Word of God is beneficial as it commands change. It has power when we release it into the atmosphere. It can destroy, heal, request grace and mercy, call out for back up, activate favour. It is a whole lot more useful than crying. Even if you have to write out the entire prayer and read it to God, could you do it? It worked for me, and it can work for you too.

The only thing new about porn is how accessible online pornography and the progressive capability of humans to amend their bodies surgically. Everything else is not new—threesomes, orgies, sex toys etc. I always wondered why God had to list the sexual do's and don't's in Leviticus. The unregenerate heart of man (without salvation) is desperately wicked.

Hebrews 10:26

"Beloved ones, let us cleans ourselves of every defilement of flesh and spirit."—2 Corinthians 7:1.

SEX

I thought about having sex while writing this book so I could share what my perspective was. I am only joking... I thought about having sex way before this book was first imagined. It is alone God's grace and mercy that restrained me. I felt it was expedient to have a more in-depth look into sex, but I did not want to spend a long time on it because I do not have a lot of personal experience. What I have done is spoken to Christian and non-Christian women who have engaged in premarital sex.

I Sara-Jayne in no way condemn or sentence anyone who is in a sexual relationship. You have free will to choose how to live your life. However, my God-given assignment is to declare that premarital sex is still a sin in 2020. My job is to talk bout the spiritual implications and consequences as well as emotional, social and mental effects. You are a spirit being living in a human body and what you do to your body matters. I can only bring the knowledge to you; you decide what happens next. I pray that you will hear the heart of your heavenly Father as you read this segment. He loves you, but He hates sin. Sin destroys what He is trying to build with you, an intimate relationship.

Some food for thought...

God designed sex. It is not just restricted to the penetrative act of sex between a man and a woman. It extends to any conscious sexual stimulation. Sex is a conscious choice to engage in erotic thought and to act on those thoughts. Pastor Tony Collins puts it like this: When married people have sex, it is a God-ordained act of worship.

"In the Old Testament, a person who wanted to get close to God went into the temple to worship. And in the deepest recess of the temple was a place called the Holy of Holies, the most sacred part of the temple was hidden behind a veil. No one could enter there but the high priest, and then only once a year with blood to cover the people's sins.

God has created every woman with a bodily veil called a hymen. This creates a covering that says what the Old Testament said about the Holy of Holies – no trespassing until it is appropriate to shed blood. That's why it is common for a woman who is still a virgin to shed blood on her wedding night. There is a breaking of the veil, the hymen, by the only person rightfully allowed to do that, the woman's husband-priest. Sexual intercourse between a husband and wife is a holy act." (8)

When you are hungry, you should eat, but when you are turned on... you do not just have sex. It is not a simple physiological behaviour. What we do to our bodies concerning eating, does not affect us in the same way as engaging in premarital sexual activity. You were not designed for sexual immorality. Any sexual activity outside the parameters God has given is immoral. Different consequences are caused by sexual sin. It goes beyond unplanned pregnancies and sexually transmitted diseases. There is a spiritual activity during the physical act. Whatever spiritual attitude the man carries; he shares it with you. Whatever spiritual condition you are in... you share it with him. No contraception can stop that spiritual activity and emotional tie you are creating.

Soul Ties

The principle of 'soul ties' is real to me. No, your souls are not bonded together literally, but there are spiritual implications to the physical act. There is a covenant or agreement that is made between the couple. Marriages can be annulled or voided if it is not consummated. Sex can be binding in earthly legal terms; so why would we be tempted to believe that in the Kingdom of God, sex is meaningless? An unauthorised sexual encounter to someone who is not your spouse will affect you spiritually. I think of a 'soul tie' as an attachment of thoughts/emotions/will.

Many use the Jonathan David thing in 1 Samuel 18 as a reference to soul ties. I do not believe it is the same bond that is created through a sexual relationship, but similar. I think this scripture refers to a highly valued friendship. It described the emotional attachment, closeness, obligation and mutual respect they had for one another. Sexual bonds, I believe, includes those determinants as mentioned above but more. It provides intimacy, vulnerability, submission to one another and susceptibility to their influence and a willingness to serve them with everything you are.

Science tells us that there are chemical changes as hormones are released through intimate physical acts. Hormones like oxytocin create a basis for bonds for relationships. Bodily actions have a psychological effect.

Although it is thought that men can have sex without any perceived emotional attachment, there are still consequences for both parties. The sex thing is so strong... I will never forget Pastor Doug William's sermon point on this subject. He shared the revelation that the 'wisest man,' 'Godliest man,' and 'strongest man;' fell to sexual sin. He was speaking about King Solomon, King David and Samson. That changed my life.

Many people get caught up on the fact that the actual phrase 'soul tie' does not appear in the Bible. We just went through a selection of scriptures about sexual integrity. We see the Bible in its entirety as being an expression of Gods heart. There is consistency in how He wants us to live. We do not need to see the words 'soul tie' to understand the significant God has placed on the union of a man and his wife. We must live righteously as the principle of sexual integrity has been demonstrated consistently.

There has GOT to be a reason God ordained sex between a man and his wife. He blesses and approves of that sexual union only. God is not mean, ignorant or stupid. He does not want to curtail our 'fun' for the sake of it. His creation assumes they know better about sex, but we do indeed reap consequences when going against His will.

We should respect the bond between man and wife as holy. That concept of 'becoming one' referenced first in Genesis 2 refers to Basar/flesh. Most assume it is just the physical representation of sex. But I believe it means more than that. The two individuals begin the process of becoming a unit. There is an attachment that keeps their marriage passionate, healthy and functional.

The three most common areas behind divorce are communication, sex and money. I cannot remember where I heard this, but in a marriage, when the sex is satisfying, it is 10% of relationship focus. When there are problems in the sexual department, it can become 90% of the relationship focus. Sex is vital within marriage, and it is the only form of relationship where God wanted it to be enjoyed.

At the end of the day, whatever your history or your current choices... there is forgiveness. There is freedom and a fresh start available. Memories attached to a sexual partner will fade. Whatever you want to call that thing that keeps you thinking about them years after, it can be broken. Renewal of the mind will follow, and you do not have to carry any shame or guilt. Who the Son (Jesus) has set free, is free indeed.

If we are truly filled with the Spirit, He must be able to influence our sexual behaviour. We must realise that holiness is more than an outward dress and religious acts. It is the posture of the heart in submission to God. A heart that has turned away and separated itself from that which offends God. It is made possible by the shed blood of Jesus that cleanses us from sin. Holiness affects how we live our lives and how we think. We have to look at sex from the standpoint of the Creator.

We must appreciate that in western society, sex has been taken out of the original context for which it was created.

There is no orgasm or relationship worth your soul. Jesus loves you and came to nail premarital sin to cross for you. If that man loves you, he will marry you first. Lust takes while love gives.

Your body is the temple of the Holy Spirit. If the man you are dealing with is not your husband, your body does not belong to him. Do not forfeit the favour of God for instant gratification. Many say premarital sex does not compare to the joy of sex within marriage. No one can tell you to abstain from sex; it is a decision you have to make for yourself having understood the Word of God for yourself. True freedom includes having a healthy sexuality.

Conclusion

Over the years, I have tried to bargain with God. Pornography becomes addictive because the journey to climax feels good, although that feeling is temporary. God asked me one day where I was planning to draw the line. I was contemplating buying a vibrator. I was deceived into thinking that my sexual needs were more significant than my need to surrender my body to God. The enemy said to me I could not live without orgasms, that it was not healthy. But this was a lie. I can, and I am living without this vice and freedom feels so good.

I know some of you have vibrators, but you do not need it. God asked me: 'what next?' Toys? Blow up dolls? Make your porn movie with you as a solo star? I remember one day having a revelation from the Holy Spirit that masturbation was a form of self-worship. He convicted me of the sin, of course, but then explained that I was not experiencing the real thing. I was experiencing a lesser grade, counterfeit, twisted version. He designed sex to be enjoyed between a husband and wife. It is not only for procreation but a symbolic act of unity, strength and intimacy.

My addiction was a short-sighted attempt to recreate a marital experience for a single person, but it ultimately left me with a more deep-seated desire for real intimacy.

The quick solo climax is counterfeit. The enemy says satisfying our sexual desires will keep lust at bay and suppress the desire for a husband. I do not care what research shows and what these new-age Christian psychologists spurt. That is a lie. Masturbation and pornography leave you with an appetite for more.

There is no middle ground, either we embrace or reject masturbation/pornography. Choose this day who you will serve. No one said being a Christian was easy, but you can walk with God in this life. It is possible to have sexual integrity, no matter how long it takes you to be free. You can be fully delivered from sexual sin if you want to. In your strength, you can do nothing, but with God, all things are possible. You first have to make up your mind to walk away.

Susanna Wesley, the mother of John Wesley (a prominent historic church leader) once wrote: "Whatever weakens your reason, impairs the tenderness of your conscience, obscures your sense of God, or takes off your relish of spiritual things; in short, whatever increases the strength and authority of your body over your mind, that thing is a sin to you, however innocent it may be in itself.' When taking the approach of purity is a posture of the heart... pornography/masturbation cannot be justified.

At one point, I prayed and asked God to take away my sexual feelings! I am glad He did not listen to me. In the case that I do meet an amazing man, I am sure he would not be pleased if I had no sex drive whatsoever. I think some women believe that asexuality is holiness... which means having no sexual feelings at all is the goal. God gave you the wiring, and the hormones, so sexual urges are not sinful in itself. The key lies in how you manage it. It can be controlled in a way that pleases the Lord. This is what I call healthy sexuality.

My future husband will also benefit from the fact that I have been delivered from a self-serving destructive addiction.

Masturbation/Pornography is self-centred. And if you can speak to wives candidly, they would tell you that there is nothing worse than a self-centred spouse in bed. Your future husband will not be able to recreate what you have been accustomed to before you were married. A wedding day does not change years of fantasy and your personal touch. Your appetite, imagination and expectations need to be refreshed before the honeymoon. Use this time during singlehood to work on this. .

When I stopped fighting God on this issue and identified it as an area of weakness, I was then free to receive His grace. He gave me the strength to break the addiction. Holy Spirit helped me identify the escape route, which may be inconspicuous but present in every temptation scenario. It has caused me to progress in my process of sanctification. I do not get it perfectly right all the time; but I know that I am now walking in more power, peace and intimacy with Christ. It is incredible how much more I can talk about in prayer when it is not entirely focused on saying 'I am sorry God, I won't do that again.' It feels incredible to be free. If you are struggling in this area, I would love to experience this freedom as well.

The Healing Process

I am going to tell you about the process I went through to overcome the addiction of masturbation/ pornography. The principles I am about to share will be useful those who desire to get out of a sexual relationship as well.

Honesty

I think the first place to start in your recovery or your comeback is honesty. You must take ownership of the addiction. Living in a state of denial is like living on ice. It is unstable and vulnerable to breaking. Ignorance is not bliss. Things only get worse if you do an ostrich and stick your head underground.

Sister, if I can get anything across in this whole book, is own your mess. Do not argue, do not try and justify. Just come clean. Face up to the facts! One thing I know God likes about me is that I put my hands up. When I had fallen to that level of rebellion where I indulged in pornography; I did not pretend it is was not a problem. I was experiencing Godly sorrow, but I do admit that I was trapped for a long while.

Feeding a pornography addiction is the fruit, but it is not the whole story. It is evidence of an unmet need (not for sex but intimacy) and unresolved issues in your life. Some of us can testify that we attempted to cut down the 'fruit', but we left the root. We rejoiced at the temporary cessation of the problem but then despaired when the behaviour returned.

Let us say, Lisa (fictional) loves attention from men and will sleep with them to make herself feel wanted. The fruit is the active pursuit of sexual escapades; the root is low self-esteem. She desires validation from men to feel like she is worth something. She may stop sleeping around one day, but because the issue of her problem has not been addressed, her willpower will fade. She will find another sexual relationship. You need to acknowledge that you have a problem before you can even begin the process of recovery.

If you do not start the process of healing/delivery when it comes to sex/masturbation/porn; you develop wilderness syndrome. This is where you metaphorically go round and round in a circle. Similar to the children of Israel after they were rescued from Egypt. What could have been a relatively brief say 40-day journey into Canaan (the promise land), took them forty years.

You do not want to die in the wilderness. What do I mean? The Holy Spirit is a gentleman, and He will not force you to choose life if you are determined to choose sin. That conscience I mentioned before will fade, and soon you will not even care that you have sinned. You may no longer hear the voice of Holy Spirit pleading to come back over the edge. In Romans 1:28 it talks about God giving man over to his reprobate mind, where they couldn't even retain the knowledge of God in their mind. That is a sorry state to be in because you do not feel the need to repent.

So be honest

- Do you have healthy sexuality?
- What habits/strongholds/practices are you struggling with?
- What are your triggers for engagement in sexual activity?
- What are your concerns about your sexual purity?
- Do you have any soul ties/emotional bonds to break from previous sexual experiences?

Inception Model

I designed a model to depict the three levels of deliverance from my addiction. I like the concept that the film Inception brought which demonstrated characters in a dream, within a dream, within a dream. To wake up, they need several kicks (a sudden trigger) to go back up the dream levels until conscious. I am going to walk you through the stages.

.

Figure 3: Sexual Sin Deliverance Model

New Normal

My turn

Supernatural
Deliverance

Level One

The Spiritual level: Supernatural Deliverance

There are no two ways to think about this. Addictions of a sexual nature have spiritual roots. You cannot bring a knife to a gunfight. Just counselling by itself... man-made positive declarations... simple willpower... is not enough. There needs to be a supernatural move of God to destroy that prison of lust. That is why honesty is essential for freedom.

When the blind man confronted Jesus, He asked him.... 'What can I do for you?' The blind man replied, 'Lord, I want to see." Jesus knew what his need was, but the blind man had to have faith to ask for deliverance. You need to ask God for deliverance from sexual sin. You cannot do it alone.

You can be a born again Christian, having accepted Christ as your Saviour but still need deliverance. Bondage is the result of whoever you have yielded yourself to. Sin can have dominion in your life even as a Christian. It requires you to break your commitment to following Christ and diverts your attention away from God... it is a master. It follows then if there is a master, there is also a slave. You will never be free if sin has mastery over you. This is the bond that needs to be broken.

> Freedom is a gift to the human race. It is the foundation of a true relationship with the Father, imparted by grace and grace alone..
> - Philip Dada Jr (Saved but Bound Course Notes) (8)

Deliverance is our right as Children of God. John 10:10 says: 'I [Jesus] have come that you may have life and life more abundantly.' Jesus died to set you free from the law of sin and death. Sin is not something you can live with if you genuinely want to live.

Freedom starts with honesty. Confess your sins to God. Agree with Him.

[1Jo 1:9 NKJV] 9 If we confess our sins, He is faithful and just to forgive us [our] sins and to cleanse us from all unrighteousness.

Repent

Just one encounter with God will change your life. He wants a relationship beyond one encounter with you, of course. But you need His power to break the neck of the addiction giant. God has to do it for you. Your role is to decide that you want to follow Him completely and humble yourself.

It is not really about your emotions, because you can be sorry and not want to change. Remorse and regret will be there; but God wants you to consciously, soberly renounce your sin. You have to want Him MORE than the temporary pleasures you have become accustomed to. This desperation will cause you to kneel in your brokenness before God.

Psalms 51 is penned beautifully by David after he had sinned with Bathsheba. But you have got to come to God as yourself. Hide nothing and express everything. It is all about faith. You must remember that your deliverance is obtained by your acceptance of what Jesus Christ did on the cross. He saved you. He took your punishment for sin. He became sin for you. Without the shedding of blood, there is no remission of sin. So God gave His Son for you to be free. Through faith, not works... you are forgiven. You then have the right to be delivered. You are not lost hope; you are God's beloved.

I cannot explain it scientifically because this is not an earthly thing. But by faith, God spiritually destroys the yoke of bondage. In one moment, He can lose you from years of abuse, sin, and addiction. It is a significant moment in the presence of the Lord. It is hard to find the words to describe the life-changing feeling of my burden being lifted off. If you struggle with sexual sin, I encourage you to experience God's grace in your area of weakness for yourself.

It is not necessarily about the big church services. It may help to have trusted sisters and mentors in the faith pray with you. You can experience a manifestation of God's power in public. You may want to jump, run, scream or fall out. However, your time of deliverance may be in your bedroom, where you are alone and still. You may feel God move upon you tangibly or you may not. But you will know that you know that your breakthrough has come. God is not moved by your religious acts, but by a heart broken over the condition of their life. Surrender to Him as you are and He will come to you.

Repentance and not penance moves the heart of Christ. You cannot earn your freedom; it is given to you. God does not want to see you suffering; He wants you free. You may want to fast and pray for this issue, to build up spiritual strength; but I promise you the deliverance

God specialises in is instant. He meets you at your point of need. No matter what you have done, His love covers it all. No matter how many times you have fallen. GET UP. GO ON. AND SIN NO MORE.

I am resisting the urge to write a prayer out because I think you should speak to God in your own way. Just be honest, Holy Spirit who confronts the sin leads us in prayer. If you want to write something down and read that is perfectly fine. You can pray using scripture. There is no formula beyond, confess and accept what Jesus did and decide that today is the day I live in freedom.

Rededicate

Now is the opportune time to rededicate your life to Christ. It is by faith or absolute belief that we are reconciled to God. When He forgives us, He throws the records/evidence of our shortcomings in the sea of forgetfulness. When we approach Him, He does not see us with our track record... He sees the blood that

Jesus shed covering us. The righteousness we wear that has wiped our slate clean was given to us by Jesus. It washes away our sins. There is now no more condemnation. You are free to move past this.

[Rom 8:1 NKJV] 1 [There is] therefore now no condemnation to those who are in Christ Jesus, who do not walk according to the flesh, but according to the Spirit.

One thing that I struggled with was the idea of forgiving myself. I held myself to a very high standard. I could not believe or accept my flaws and mistakes. But I understand now that you must release yourself. Regularly rehearsing the past, berating yourself, punishing yourself denies the finished work of Christ. You must forgive yourself. The accuser of the brethren, also known as the Devil, will be quick to make you doubt your deliverance. You shut him down with your profession of faith. 'Christ Jesus has set me free!' Do not join him in slinging mud. If God says it is time to move on, you must move on.

> [Phl 3:13 NKJV] 13 Brethren, I do not count myself to have apprehended; but one thing [I do], forgetting those things which are behind and reaching forward to those things which are ahead.

During deliverance, at that moment, God breaks soul ties (emotional and spiritual bonds). He restores your purity and peace of mind. He releases you from the cycle of sin. He casts demonic spirits like lust and shame out of your life. He silences the enemy who seeks to intimidate and oppress. Wherever shame is hiding, He shines and brings you into His presence. There is nothing that can compare to being delivered. The grace of God comes like a light sabre to cut through the chains to a sexual relationship. God strips away the authority of sin to keep you hostage. He says run... I got you covered. The door is open, and now YOU have to walk through it.

Level Two

The Natural Level: My Turn

So here we are. God has supernaturally broken the power of sin in your life. This is awesome! God deserves all the praise, accolades and worship for this from you. However, now it is your turn again to move forward in your freedom.

You have the mind of Christ
It is with the mind or will that we serve the Lord. Paul prayed that we might have the same mind, which was in Christ Jesus. Jesus went through the same temptations we experience and released power to resist them on us. When He was tempted in the Wilderness by the Devil (see Luke 4); He did not defeat the Devil as the Son of God. Follow me.

You have the Holy Spirit and the Word
When Jesus was on earth in the flesh, he had the power to use His supernatural abilities to put that foe in

his place. However, everything He did on earth. He did as a man filled with the Holy Spirit. The human side of Jesus was filled with the Holy Spirit without measure. (We have just a measure!) He purposefully wanted to demonstrate how to respond when confronted by the enemy in times of weakness.

How did He respond? He used the Word of God to rebuke that serpent. He did not get into a debate with the Devil. He knew the truth of God and declared the truth of God. Each time the Devil came to him with something crazy, he clapped back: IT IS WRITTEN!

The Devil will try and make you think that the deliverance did not work. Or make you feel that you are bound to relapse. But you stand your ground by declaring what God says. It is written: if the Son sets you free, you will be free indeed. [Jhn 8:36 NIV]

To maintain your sexual integrity, your mind must be DAILY renewed with the Word of God. (Rom 12:1-2,

Phil 4:8) Psalms 119: Thy word have I hid in my heart that I might not sin against thee.

Make a Bible study out of what God says about love, purity and singlehood. When you saturate your mind in scriptures, it builds spiritual strength to withstand the pressure from the enemy. Daily renew your mind to filter out all the rubbish you have encountered throughout the day that seeks to undermine God's truth.

Speak Life

My advice for those coming out of sex-related addiction; is to prepare ten statements about your freedom. You need daily affirmation that will build you up in times when you feel as if you cannot withstand the pressure. Even though you are delivered, expect to be tested. There will be push back from the enemy. He has lost his foothold in your life, and he will fight to regain it. We will not allow it! Like that Gandalf in Lord of the Rings we holler, 'you shall not pass!!'

For example

- ➤ The shame I feel when I masturbate is not worthwhile. I do not want to bring this into my marriage
- ➤ I rather wait for my husband to have sex
- ➤ I have been down this road before; it does not lead anywhere good
- ➤ This temptation has a way to escape. I do not have to sin
- ➤ [Gal 5:1 NIV] It is for freedom that Christ has set us free. Stand firm, then, and do not let yourselves be burdened again by a yoke of slavery

… And so on.

I have a few sheets of a paper in my bedroom with scriptures, statements and positive declaration. These prepared statements and declarations help me shut down dialogue with the enemy. The Word of God has the power, so naturally, my affirmations that come from the Word also has power. I speak life unto myself and prepare for things to live.

It is so important to have a pure thought process because as a man thinks in His heart so is He (Proverbs 23:7.) You win the battle in your mind first before it is lived out in earthly reality. So if you entertain lustful thoughts, you will find yourself returning to your vomit. No more! Say goodbye to bondage and that horrible sin cycle.

Tear down strongholds

There are other practical things you must do to stand fast in the liberty wherein Christ has made you free. You have to learn how to be master over your own body. This starts by pulling down strongholds.

Strongholds were taught to me to be a faulty system of thinking (leading to behaviour) derived from a carnal (fleshy) or demonic source. So it might go like this: I am only human. I am unable to control my sexual urges. I live in a world that tells me to 'just do it.' The Bible is old fashioned and out of touch with modern times. Engaging in sexual sin is not the worse sin, and God will forgive me anyhow. These problematic thoughts need to be deal with. This does not necessarily happen during the Level One deliverance time. This is a second phase where I must actively engage in pulling down 'wrong thinking.'

Or it may go like this: I am tired of being lonely. I do not want to end up alone, and I have no other decent choices. Bobby (fictional) makes me feel valued. I will have sex with Bobby because he said that he wants to marry me. God must not mind because nothing bad has happened since we started sleeping together. Everyone is doing it. I am normal. This pattern of thinking is stronghold.

[2 Co 10:4-5 NIV] 4 The weapons we fight with are not the weapons of the world. On the contrary, they have divine power to demolish strongholds. 5 We demolish arguments and every pretension that sets itself up against the knowledge of God, and we take captive every thought to make it obedient to Christ.

We pull down strongholds bit by bit. This prevents us going back into what we have been delivered from. You may need counselling help with this. You may need to construct a fasting and prayer schedule to focus on sexual integrity. You may need to intentionally work on building your self esteem to a healthy level.

[Eph 4:22-24 NIV] 22 You were taught, with regard to your former way of life, to put off your old self, which is being corrupted by its deceitful desires; 23 to be made new in the attitude of your minds; 24 and to put on the new self, created to be like God in true righteousness and holiness.

Clean up

You cannot.... You cannot... you cannot keep your environment the same but expect your life to be different. There are some physical triggers for sexual sin you need to remove quick time. Sit down in a quiet moment and make a list of everything you consider a temptation for this and how you plan to tackle it. I will repeat this: I will be tested so I will prepare for confrontation.

Keenly monitor your eye, ear and mouth gate. There may be movies to throw out, pictures of crushes to delete, music that needs to erased. These things take you to a mental place where you no longer entertain sexually explicit thoughts. Sexually charged atmospheres attempt to draw you back into bondage.

Observe the company you keep as they can influence your morality. There will always be social pressure, but you can limit the time you remain in the fire. You have a right not to be bombarded with sexually explicit ideas at school, college and work. Redirect conversation, have several friends or groups of people you can choose to sit with over a meal. Recognise who is helping your spiritual growth and who is harming it. Make changes accordingly; your spiritual welfare is more important than popularity.

Clear off

An essential strategy behind escaping temptation is to run. Opportunity to return to your old life will present itself. You need an emergency plan to getaway. Even though you are delivered from the bondage of sin, in Level Two, you are still vulnerable to that temptation. The best way to fight this particular battle is to run.

If it is a case of being tempted to masturbate or watch porn; you could put on worship music, go for a run, phone a friend (a mature friend of the same sex, not a man) or put on a comedy to make yourself laugh. You need to distract yourself and occupy your time with something else you enjoy.

You do not need to worry about being strong at all times. You are not continuously tested throughout the day. There are just moments of weakness you have to deal with. A sexual thought may come into your mind, in a split second, you decide whether you entertain it or bounce your mind unto one of your affirmations.

That ex calls, the one that made love to you the way you liked it; now you have to decide whether to answer or block his number. It is these times that you need to show strength. These tests require a quick response to pull yourself out of the fire. However, my advice is to prepare for war in times of peace.

Try not to make the mistake of overestimating what you can handle. Sexual sin is one of the only things the Bible tells us to run from.

Runaway from the very appearance evil. (1 Thess 5: 22) Much like Joseph, who left his coat in Potiphar's wife's hands. Yes, what guy did to girl in Chapter one of this book. Level Two actions may involve going things that you used to like. Let us be very real; you may have to leave a relationship if the guy you are dating does not want to give up sex. If he is constantly testing your boundaries, it comes down to making a choice. I want to encourage you that what you are walking towards is more powerful than what you left behind. You know what going back to those sinful habits feels like and it is not worth it.

Level 2 is also about healing. God does not want you walking around with patches, but He would like to restore you. He embraces you in your journey and calls you daughter. Understand you belong in His family. You have value no matter what your testimony is. Do not allow anybody to cause you to feel unworthy because of where you have come from. Your name is 'blessed and highly favoured by' God.

Level Three

Maintenance: The New Normal

Level Three is built on top of Level Two. In Level Three, after a while, you find the intensity of old temptations reduces. The memories of your former lifestyle fade with time. The work that the Word is doing in your character gets your life into shape. You are delivered, and now you are healed. You become more astute at recognising triggers and adapt your life to avoid them. You may notice you can tolerate more and not think about going back to sexual sin. Celebrate this achievement because God has worked a miracle. Your sin was meant to take you out, but you had the audacity to fight. This is a great position to be in, but it is not over. There is another Level to your freedom walk.

Pastor YPJ has a beautiful sermon where he demonstrates how a believer becomes entangled in sin then delivered from it. He addresses our triune nature: Body, Soul and Spirit. We are meant to live from Spirit to Soul to the body. But when we become disconnected from God, it flips the order. We live for the body and its needs which can cause significant issues with a walk with God. So how do you reconnect with God? How do you remain in submission to His Holy Spirit?

Spiritual Discipline

Jesus spoke about the fact that once an evil spirit leaves a house if it comes back to finds the house empty, he will return with several spirits worst than himself. (Luke 11:24 - 26) I have interpreted this to mean my home, my life; my time must be occupied with the things of God. After being delivered, you respond by making changes to your environment and healing. This then must be followed by creating a new normal.

You need to be engaged with things that build your spiritual muscle. Athletes follow the same principle. They adopt a very intentional and disciplined holistic approach to their life. They have to be disciplined if they are going to be effective in their sport—Champions train.

Train? Discipline? Build? All the words that make you tired just looking at them. Israel Houghton sang: 'I'm not going back, I'm moving ahead, I'm here to declare to you the past is over...' Yet, what keeps you moving ahead is discipline. You do not want to relapse; you want to progress.

The spiritual disciplines are essential for maintaining your victory. They do not talk about this much at church conferences. You often leave a big service fired up and ready to punch the Devil in the eye. Two days later, you are back down from your emotional high and into the same old drama. It takes effort to walk with God.

Routine prayer, praise and worship, fasting, reading the Word, engaging with a spirit-filled church, build your spiritual strength. These things are the ingredients for success. It is your responsibility to move beyond surviving to thrive as a Christian. No one can do it for you. You have your relationship with God. You may have to make a mental move from just loving God to being in love with God. Develop an appreciation for resting His presence like you would your future husband. Long to hear His voice and to know His heart.

You build a relationship with God like any other relationship. You need lots of communication and quality time spent together. I emphasise the Word quality as I am guilty of rushing God. I may multitask speaking to Him and preparing food. It is ok to talk to God throughout the day but does He have preeminence in your life? Does He have a particular time where you two meet? I had to work on this myself over the years. It is nothing to spend 5 hours watching an exciting Netflix show... binge binge binge! But it seems little over the top to spend 5 hours in prayer. No! That is not right. It is the Devil's tactic to keep you weak and ignorant of your potential in Christ. Treat God with the knowledge that you are living life IN Him, not around Him. He wants personal involvement and time set aside for your relationship.

Call on the Holy Spirit. The Holy Spirit dwells within us, but if you are not filled with the Holy Spirit, seek the overflow anointing that He brings. This will empower you with supernatural strength. This strength comes in handy when caught in a tempting situation. Do not ignore the Holy Spirit or restrict His work to just a Sunday. Learn about Him also as the Comforter and seek to know Him better. He will give you wisdom and guide you into all truths. He will provide you with the signal when a situation is going to get out of control. He was sent by Jesus to empower the believer to live an abundant life as a witness for the Kingdom.

Spend time in worship. This gives us access to a secret place in God where you do not have to worry about what your flesh is doing. Psalms 91 says He that lives in the secret place of the Most High shall remain under the shadow of the almighty. In God's presence, you can draw down strength, peace, relaxation and relief from the pressures of life. We were created primarily to worship God. When we lose ourselves in worship, our connection to God is strengthened.

Submerse yourself in fun activities. Sis! Keep your life full, exciting and productive. Having too much time on your hands is not a good thing. Go travelling, take up a new challenge, find new hobbies and take care of your physical body. Exercise is an essential component of my life now. Those energy-consuming activities release tension and stress carves out a tighter figure and improves my overall health. It is a win, win, win situation.

Accountability

Be open about your battle with sexual sin with trusted mature people, who can support you and encourage you if you feel weak. Sometimes you need the power of agreement in prayer. Other times you need encouragement, just someone to say it is going to be alright. You can do all things through Christ, but you do not need to do all things alone. I understand that it may be hard to trust at times when you have been hurt in the past. However, I believe God will provide friends and support for you. You need a safe place where you can speak freely without judgement. I can provide some form of help through the Adam Meet Eve Agency.

I believe in the power of prayer, and I know that people prayed for me. At the most random times, I feel a strong wave of strength and joy. I believe it is in response to the prayer of friends. The spiritual realm is always active. The enemy does not rest, and neither should we when it comes to prayer.

[Jas 5:16 NKJV] 16 Confess [your] trespasses to one another, and pray for one another, that you may be healed. The effective, fervent prayer of a righteous man avails much.

[Gal 6:1-2 NKJV] 1 Brethren, if a man is overtaken in any trespass, you who [are] spiritual restore such a one in a spirit of gentleness, considering yourself lest you also be tempted. 2 Bear one another's burdens, and so fulfil the law of Christ.

There is strength in unity with the body of Christ. It may be wise not to share your story while you are still going through your healing with the general public. However select a power-filled team that can carry you, much like the four friends who brought the paralytic man into the presence of Jesus. The right friends can support by checking in and cheering you on.

Conclusion

When my addiction to porn was broken, I realised that my attitude towards God had changed. It was not how much I could get away with, but it was how much I could stay close to Christ. I chose to honour the Word of God for what it is... truth. In the past, I tried to justify my sin, but I stopped looking for loopholes to continue offensive behaviour. I stopped aiming for the minimum requirement of holiness. (Does not even exist.) My old attitude, although I was Christian, was stinky. It set me for failure in the battle for sexual purity.

[Isa 11:2 NKJV] 2 The Spirit of the LORD shall rest upon Him, The Spirit of wisdom and understanding, The Spirit of counsel and might, The Spirit of knowledge and of the fear of the LORD.

I now promote HEALTHY sexuality. I try not to encourage women to ignore or suppress that which God gave them as apart of their human experience. Your sexual nature is a part of you; it does not just appear on your wedding day. It just needs to be managed, and carefully so, during singlehood.

Some Christian women who struggle to attract men; do so because they have suppressed their sexuality. They hide their femininity and physique, leaving nothing appealing for the men to be attracted to. I am not interested in a guy who is not physically attracted to me.

These women may dress in a way that is simply a turn-off. They are not friendly with single guys. They do not know how to speak in a pleasant sweet manner which would intrigue a single man. No..., this is not of God. Dressing in a way that flatters your figure does not have to be revealing. You should feel comfortable speaking to men in a pleasant manner. Wearing heels does not make you a Jezebel. Your sexuality or femininity can be expressed in a way that honours God.

The temptation is not the sin, i.e. being turned on is not the sin; the sin is what you do next. 1 Cor 10:13 – With every temptation, there is a way of escape. Holy Spirit will reveal the escape in every situation.

My final piece of advice to this chapter is that you have to be realistic. I found that I had terrible days, but I appreciated that there were more often good days in my faith walk. Should you mess up, confess, repent and GET UP. Jesus will forgive your sin and cleanse you from all unrighteousness. Even if you make a big mistake or relapse, God will not give up on you, so NEVER give up on yourself. Be defiant in the face of opposition. You will win!

Chapter Six

_____Mock Trials_____

On a cloudy Thursday, I was expecting rain... nope. It was a Sunday. It was a sunny Sunday in spring. I met Pinch. A mutual friend had given me a warning shot that I would meet this wonder of a man called Pinch. I raised an eyebrow at some of the achievements. Yes, I conceded, he sounded like quality, but I was genuinely sceptical. When I first saw him, I was like who is this random guy who looks like he blew in from simpleville? Anyways, right from the get, I noticed that Pinch rated himself. His confidence caught my attention, and the banter was good. Some guys like eye contact and then there is Pinch. I felt like he was looking into my soul. I was interested. It was an excellent first meet as far as introductions go.

One thing you need to know about Pinch is that he is far from simple; he was/is scarily intelligent, perceptive and witty. I realised very quickly that his mind was a supercomputer and nothing gets past him. I think it is his most attractive and intriguing characteristic. A few weeks later, a bunch of us went to the movies. The one thing my baby sister said was not to sit next to him. So naturally, I sat next to him in true Sj fashion.

All God told me about Pinch was to wait, but I was not confident that it meant it was going to work out in my favour. This was new territory for me; I had met someone that I thought was equal. The FIRST person ever I considered an equal to myself. He brought what I needed from a man to the table. Spiritually... the maturity was there; I could palpate his passion for God. Family... he was dedicated to caring for those he loved. He told me things that reassured me that he would make an excellent Father. He was not a model let me put it that way, but he was tall. It was as if my lottery number had just been called.

You ladies may know what it is like to meet someone you felt was 'the one for you." The actual person with many of the qualities you have been looking for in a man. It was as if God has taken some scissors and cut him out of my dreams. He did not look like what I thought my future husband should have looked like, but he sure sounded like him. I went nuts. I lost my sanctified mind. Everything I thought I had learnt about keeping cool, going with the flow, flew out the window along with the guard around my heart.

Pinch did this thing where he would anticipate what I was saying before I said it. He put it down to having a sister, but wherever he learnt it, it was a dangerous turn on. I understood the gravitas of his dreams, and his life was going in a direction I could support. I could almost hear his brain ticking over trying to work me out. And it felt good to be a puzzle that a good man wanted to figure out. I liked the attention, and I was flattered by the interest. I did not go looking for it, so it was a welcome surprise. Was this my when-I-was-not-looking for-him-my-husband found me storytime?

You see, I thought I had completed all my practices and made all my mistakes. I had already checked out of the singlehood academy and bought my wedding dressing dress (figuratively) for graduation. I felt like he was the actual one for me. The unpredictable meeting, super cool chemistry, underlying intrigue and attraction. It all was adding up. However, when I factored in the combination of his hesitancy and God's silence, it drove me mad.

Whenever you ask God a question be prepared for yes, no or wait. It was the wait that was the worse. At least with the first two, you can process and respond. I felt like the wait response put my life on pause. So even though my circumstances were on pause, my emotions were not. I fell in love quickly with the idea that this man was mine. No matter what I did... I could not ruin it because... this was it.

Unfortunately, ladies, to give you the long story short.... it did not work out. I could write a chapter of 10,000 words on how I felt like something you flushed away in a toilet. It was embarrassing. I started this book several years ago; I was hoping to end this book with big news. My plan was to encourage you all with my testimony that had a traditionally sweet ending. I would have been all "Look how God came through for me! Won't He do it? Won't He will?" You would say: "Well if Sara works through her issues and then meet the guy of her dreams. I can too." I wanted to give you that Hollywood ending. We all get happy and get married—the end.

Well... this is reality. Wake up! Plot twist! We went from "you are the most amazing woman I have ever met" and "I just need time to sort things out in my life." With a little "You are the woman, I seriously considered to be my wife, I have spoken to my mum about you." All the way to "I can see your spiritual side, but I cannot see your personality." "Your behaviour was too erratic, and I kept trying to calm you down to see your personality behind, but I could not find it." I did not make any promises to you." "It would not be best for us to be friends as you have developed an emotional attachment." And no, I will not go to this concert with you; the one you told me about and invited me to. But I will show up with some other people and completely ignore your existence.

So much happened in such a short space of time. It showed me where I was still getting stuck. My foundation in singlehood was not stable. I was still HOPEbroken and as a result; I got manhandled, confused by myths and bogged down in a big ol' mudhole. It took a little while to get over it because I was extremely disappointed with what appeared to be the last train of the night at the time. I thought he was my only opportunity for marriage.

I wanted to include this story because it supports everything I have been rattling on about in previous chapters. At the time, I did not have the wisdom, or instead I did not follow the wisdom that I am now sharing with you. Do not make the same mistakes I did.

By the way, I had to accept his rejection without rejecting myself. You must do the same.

Post mortem

Although we never officially went on a single date (according to him), it was the most significant situationship I had experienced in my 20s. Ideally, everyone needs someone in their life to help them deal with the aftermath of a broken situation. We are women! We process our thoughts out loud. That is why we talk so much. While men will ponder in their cave, we prefer a cup of strong tea and some intelligent conversation.

This is an extreme example but humour me so I can use the analogy. If you have ever separated from someone unexpectedly, it is like an unexplained death. And when someone dies suddenly, it is custom that the specialists do a post mortem. The coroner wants to know what happened.

There is nothing wrong with talking about your situation through. My advice is, to be honest, and prepare to discover some hard truths. Hindsight is a detailed but also a harsh teacher. You may have been moving so fast that the red flag became a red blur, easy to forget. Analysis can help you to learn and move past the situation. The disclaimer is that you may not get all the answers as there are times when the secrets are locked in the guys head. Who knows what they were thinking? Who knows if what they told you was the truth?

Closure is something you need to learn how to achieve by yourself. I tried to do a closure session with Pinch months after he pulled the plug. He hijacked the meeting and left me more confused than when I first sat down. It was not helpful in the slightest. I did it because I always like to give my benediction, the last words, the final thought; but in some situations, it is not worth it lol. Let it be. Let it die. Commit that situation to the ground. Throw some flowers and take a deep breath. You are still alive, and there is better hope for tomorrow.

If you do not mind, I would like you to be my accountability person so I can show you how it works... go ahead and ask me these three questions.

...ARE YOU OVER HIM?

Am I over him? I believe I am. I was HOPEbroken, but I am pleased to report that I came through the other side. I wish I did not pursue and pressure him as I did. It is almost like apologising for a child spilling a drink on the floor, at a young age its understandable for them to make those mishaps. I still had my child-like mentality hat on when it came to matters of the heart, and so my attitude towards Pinch was understandable. It was sad because I would have expected more of myself. The wisdom has now fully downloaded. He gave me the final kick needed to bring me back up to reality; my dreidel has stopped spinning, I am enjoying living in the real world.

.... ARE YOU WHOLE?

How many know you can be "over a situation" but not healed from it? Many jump into another situation with their broken pieces.

Initially, just after it happened, I cried a lot. I am the weeping prophet and boy can I weep! I remember lying on the floor playing "Christ is enough for me" on repeat for about an hour. This was the closest I got to a being in a real relationship, and he had sooooooo many qualities I was looking for. I told you, I thought it was my one opportunity for love and I ruined it with impatience and immaturity.

I know Pinch would never admit to his part, because of his built-in constructive criticism deflector. When one is always right, one does not need the ability to listen; there is no need to learn. But his social methodology was not right, and he created the expectations that he could not and did not want to fulfil. I am not responsible for who is attracted to me, but I am responsible for who I entertain. His behaviour was hurtful, and I lost a lot of confidence.

Recovery from that romantic debacle took time; I had to get over the HOPEbroken season. The coming out process required me to own up to the things I did not do right and work with God to fix it. Working on this book was apart of my therapy. I had to go back into my past, find the root, confront some profound truths and get those myths out of my head. I spoke with God, read His word and applied it like Canadian healing oil to my emotional bruises.

When God said that He desires truth in the inward part to David, it means ensuring what you believe about yourself matches up to what God says about you. I learnt to love myself because I started to understand who I was in God. I made myself a promise not to put myself into that vulnerable position again.

If that was my only opportunity for love (it is not), I did the best I could at the time. And even though that man rejected me, I now know without a shadow of a doubt that I am a good woman. I deserve real love; I deserved to be valued, to be treated with respect. And I honestly rather be alone than to be with someone who does not feel the same way. I have never before believed I deserved the right person, so I thought I had to make do with whatever crumbs fell by my idea. I destroyed that lie like Luke Cage destroys buildings. That desperation is gone.

....WHAT EXACTLY DID YOU LEARN?
One of my favourite preachers Bishop Sean Teal said once: that God is not just interested in the final destination but the journey of your life. I scribbled as I sat down cross-legged one day, not easy for a bigger girl and made a list.)

- ➤ Not to open my heart to a man who has not opened his heart to me
- ➤ To never pursue a man. NEVER!

➤ That prayer and fasting are correct. It will help me hear God. But there is no point listening if I am not going to obey what He says.

➤ A man who wants you will NOT encourage you 'to consider other men' despite the fact 'he has not excluded the possibility of "us" That is a player language for: "I think you are cool, but you are just an option. Not a strong one at that." Or he would whisk you off the market.

➤ I did not have confidence in myself to think I deserved to be treated better.

➤ I did not believe that I was worthy of a good man.

➤ A man can be successful in one area of his life, but not be able to lead a relationship in an honourable way.

➤ If he is into you, he may not have time, but he will MAKE time for you.

➤ Do not say "God said" unless you know God said. Because God does not lie, and He is also not the author of confusion.

➢ God said, can change to God had said and is now saying. I.e. Abraham kill your son Issac. Abraham stop, there is a ram in the thicket. You just got to keep listening.

➢ Never reply when angry. Delete the first ten versions or so. Emotions will explode and fade away, and you cannot take back what you said.

➢ A man has free will; he can be presented with a gift and NOT take it.

➢ My value in God's eyes is not determined by how many men pursue me.

➢ I will stick with God even when I am low in faith.

➢ Faith can be depleted and has to be renewed by the Word of God.

➢ Pinch is not the one for me because he did not want me. It does not matter how many great qualities he has. He cannot be considered as the one for me due to his disengagement. So if marriage is in God's will for me, there will be another man far greater who wants me

➢ I have to forgive and let go until all the negativity has passed from my emotions.

➢ I have to be the best me, for me.

Aesha Adams wrote one of the most helpful articles on the planet. It is about how to recognise a good potential without supernatural signs. Do check it out! (9)

I am sure I did things that I was not proud of, that contributed to the speed at which the situation combusted. When I am upset, I will turn wolverine quickly with my words can cut worst than his razors. You would be pleased to know I have apologised for my part.

In the end, Pinch acknowledged my displeasure over the whole thing, and IF he did anything to offend me, he was sorry. IF you know... that built-in criticism deflector works so well. I sincerely wish Pinch all the best and pray that he finds who is looking for.

If you have ever been through a time of disappointment, ask yourself those three questions. Write down the answers in your diary and be specific, honest and transparent. It will help open dialogue between you and God. Your relationship needs to be strengthened now and more than ever. He will cocoon you in His presence and restore your soul. Anything you lost, even if you had sex with the guy; God will go to work like a surgeon, cutting soul ties and giving you back the parts of your heart you gave away. He will breathe new life into your dreams, passions and remind you of your purpose.

Your life is not over. It does not matter how many people are glad that it did not work out. No matter the fact you have to switch your Facebook status back or delete pictures. Clear out your phone and make room for your future. Whatever you need to do move on, girl do it, for the best is yet to come.

Chapter Seven

___The Ultimate Breakthrough___

Do you remember when I said that I wanted to end this book with good news? Well, I have it. I have had THE BREAKTHROUGH—the most significant progression since committing my heart to Christ. When I started this book in 2011, I was collating data, some of it was going into my head, but I had not truly grasped the full truth of what God was saying to me.

I was trapped in this destructive cycle of HOPEbrokeness, and it took the power of God to break it. When He did, I finally got the healing of my heart that I needed and it changed me forever. This is the spiritual and psychological freedom that women around the world are looking for. It is mega! It is huge! It is like flipping the switch on and chasing every drop of darkness out of the door. Life is still not perfect, I have many questions about the future, but I have never been so satisfied and settled.

Something clicked. That devilish lie that had been haunting my mind had been evicted. I looked in the mirror and embraced the woman looking back at me; with all her flaws, rejection and craziness. I fell in love with myself. I finally accepted what God has been saying about me my whole life. I believed Him when He said I was worthy of respect. The basic life truths that are fundamental for healthy self-esteem has now fully formed. God healed my eyes. He healed my mind and healed my heart.

I was delivered from the perception that I had a curse on my love life. Not true. It is not right for any of us. None of us is built for a life full of disappointment and heartache. There may be chapters of unexpected tragedy, but it is not the end of the story. We are being set up for a significant victory because we belong to a God who is Lord over everything.

When God clears your spiritual house of emotional junk and spiritual burden, the Holy Spirit fills you up with His fruit (Gal 5:22) and His Gifts (1 Cor 14).

Finally, He had space to fill my entire life with His presence. I was no longer focused on trying to be my saviour.

The Holy Spirit gave me the gift of a positive mindset, and as a knock-on effect, my entire perspective on life changed. For someone who was a former realist {dressed up pessimist} this was no small feat. Precepts I was reading in the Bible, words people had given me, life lessons now made more sense to me. I stopped fighting God and started accepting His love as the only love I needed to thrive. This renewal of mind transformed my entire life.

1) I am content with singlehood
2) I can accept that I am a good woman who would be an excellent blessing to a good man
3) I will not entertain a man who treats me less than a Queen
4) Joy is a gift of the spirit which is not attached to my circumstances
5) It is possible to maintain my sexual integrity

6) It is okay for me to have the desire for marriage and love God fully

7) Even if I do not get married, I will have a remarkable life

These are my genuine declaration of beliefs coming from the bottom of my heart. Having this fundamental foundation, I find that I am a much more balanced woman. For the first time in my life, I am not running around trying to seek validation. I know who I am in God, and I completely trust His leadership over my life.

What are your declarations?

You can't believe those seven statements written above and be HOPEbroken. HOPEbrokenness is not your portion. Whatever your story is, regardless of how awful it is, it has no power to hold you back from becoming all God ordained you to be. This next chapter of your life is about your strength and victory. You do not have to make the same mistakes before because the cycle is broken.

I used to feel that as a single woman, my most significant breakthrough would be to have a husband. But it is not, and I do not pray that as my first prayer for myself or other single women anymore. It is not getting that sought after engagement ring or finally being able to post pictures/videos on your social media with you and 'bae.'

The most significant achievement is to be genuinely content as you are alone and not losing your faith that God can provide a husband for you. It is to go through your process of healing and maturation. It is to acquire every drop of wisdom from previous experiences, genuinely loving and appreciating your awesomeness. It is about believing what God says about you and what He is doing for you. Your peace is protected from pressure coming from previous broken relationships, family, friends and media. It is having JOY in the season of singlehood!

Today I metaphorically reach back into your past; I pull down every harmful myth and lie over your life. You are who God says you are. You are not what men who have mistreated you have called you. You are worthy of love and respect. You have a unique purpose for being on this earth, and you will achieve it. You have every right to be free and to enjoy the days' God has blessed you with. I stand with you, shoulder to shoulder, and we march towards the future.

I pray for complete healing of your mind, body and soul: no missing pieces, no exposed scar, no confusion. Let the peace of God that surpasses all understanding guard your heart and thoughts. You are not alone, and God is going to walk you through the difficult seasons that will come to you as a single woman. You are guaranteed to make it if you do not let go of God's hand. His hand will guide, cover and provide for you.

The Lord is your ultimate shepherd, and you will want for nothing. I boast on God's ability to keep you happy because He has been an excellent Shepherd over me.

Am I married? ...Not even close. But I did not need to get married to get the love, security, affirmation, excitement and fulfilment I was looking for. I have all that and more right at this very moment. When He chooses to provide, my future husband will ADD to my pre-existing joy. There will be such purpose to our union that it makes sense for us to be together.

You have everything you need to be happy right at this moment. Contentment in Christ does not come from your circumstances, but it is born at the moment you decide to believe His Word. Do not waste another second feeling sorry for yourself because you are single. Breathe in the freedom and live life at maximum volume. No more being negatively manhandled, no more myths and no more mudholes.

FIGHT FOR IT

I should have known that once you have had the breakthrough, you have to maintain it. Even when you have progressed, you are guaranteed to encounter new challenges. Life will not feel like sunshine and ice cream every day. Maybe you meet another man, and it feels like the same thing is happening again. Another mudhole? What if you mess up again? What if you relapse back into negative thoughts? Another Myth! If you are like me, then your first reaction is to isolate yourself to minimise shame. But I encourage you Woman of God, do not be ashamed to talk with God.

Do not isolate yourself from your heavenly Father. He has seen and heard it all, and you are not alone. Talk to God about everything. The key thing in maintaining your deliverance is keeping memories of your progress alive. Remember back in Chapter Two when I said it was good to mark any achievement? That picture, holiday, journal entry serves as a monument. You look at it whenever you need to and reflect on the work God has done in your life. If He did it before, He would deliver you again.

I reckon that we have a choice. We can either choose to stumble through our singlehood season however long it lasts, or we could be successful and excel beyond our dreams. I have chosen the latter. I am not going to mislead you; it takes work to keep focused. I have to intentionally invest in my relationship with God to keep myself out of trouble. The war on sexual integrity alone is relentless, and every day we are engaged in battle. I am not going down a loser, so... I use the weapons of warfare made mighty through Christ.

Weapon ONE: WORSHIP

Real spirit and truth worship translate you into God's presence. Heaven touches earth right where you are, and you will feel a manifest presence. You don't need to chant, or adopt a position, nor rearrange your room. God, the true living God, comes when His children call Him. There is nothing more attractive to Him than worship. When we worship Him for who He is without all our desires being fulfilled, it means we are genuine. This is sincere praise and worship. Intentionally, prioritise what He wants, which is your time and adoration, and you appreciate how well God faithfully takes care of your needs.

Weapon TWO: PRAYER

When I pray, I pray scriptures because you remind God of His WordWord. Sometimes we do not receive because we do not ask effectively. No, it is not the length of prayer, and sometimes all you can do is cry. But when you provide evidence to God that He promised something, He responds. His WordWord has He exalted above His name. There are over 300 promises to us in the Bible; you have every right as a child of God to claim them. So if you are going to pray about singlehood then pray the WordWord. I find scriptures that support my prayers and present it to God with confidence.

I am so much better when I am in communication with Him. He helps you get through the day. The enemy does not rattle your emotions so easily. Constant communication and awareness of His presence in my mundane everyday activities has helped to maintain my positive mind-set.

JESUS IS NOT MY BOYFRIEND!

I think the idea of dating God is a bit strange, but I do get what people mean when they say that Jesus is their boyfriend. I am sure all it is, is spending some quality time to build a more meaningful relationship. God is not your boyfriend or husband, though. Often it is those women who are the most lonely and sad about their status.

God is not my man; I would like to be blessed with an actual husband. God has not and will not climb into any bed with any woman. He created marriage for a good reason. I do like taking walks and speaking to God. I love singing to Him; I like listening to Him. I like watching sermons/bible studies on Youtube and pausing and discussing it with God. I have purposefully got into the habit of addressing Him first thing in the morning (instead of the phone grab) and making sure we have quiet time at night. However, the husband position is very vacant.

Weapon THREE: FAITH

Faith is the substance of things hoped for the evidence of things not seen. If you can see something, then you do not need faith. Your faith WILL be tested. You will be dropped in situations that directly oppose the promises God made you. FULLY opposite. Can you still believe?

My spirit has to keep hearing God despite my circumstances, screaming into the ears of my soul. Can you ignore what you see? Instead, choose to tune in and focus on what God promised? I find that I get so tired. Let us keep it real; we are human. So my strategy is to block up my ears with the Word. It is the devil's job to bombard you with his weapons of destruction so you need to fight back by submerging yourself in things that will build your faith.

I believe you have to DAILY renew your faith. Faith is a gift from God. The Bible says you only need faith as small as a mustard seed to move mountains; I realise that faith comes in measures. Faith can be grown by hearing and believing the Word of God.

Weapon Four: FRIENDSHIP

Surround yourself with positivity. I had to lock down my friendship circle. I love everyone and can hang out with people in group settings fine. But I realise not everyone should be in the inner circle. Those I choose to get close, must be people worthy of my trust; they respect me and bring something positive. I need encouragers, not haters. It is not self-centred to guard the guest list to your private life. The friends you choose in this season should challenge you to come up higher. You want to be inspired and accountable to these individuals. People who will support your maintaining your sexual integrity and being the best woman you can be on your own.

> People are known for the company they keep. Birds of a feather flock together. It is easier to pull someone down than lift them up. If your friends are obsessed with desperately chasing men, chances are you will be dragged in by peer pressure to do it too. Make the right decisions because they can influence you in your social life.

Weapon FIVE: HONESTY

I would be lying if I told you that I liked being single every day. I do not, just plain and simple. I have to be honest with God. I am allowed to have my moments as long as I do not let the moment to have me. I acknowledge, take a moment to vent and then move on. If I am not feeling great... I tell God... I tell my friends. I do not have to be superwoman 24/7. It is not possible to be perfect, and the energy it takes to keep up that charade is unsustainable. I am not competing in a race for anyone or trying to impress them. I am determined to complete the path set before me by God at my own pace.

WEAPON SIX: TRUTH

I do not entertain lies. When a negative thought enters my mind, I do not ignore it. No matter how small or large, I actively reject the idea before it plants itself. I do this by declaring a positive thing to counteract the negative.

For example, a couple walks past me.
Negative thought: She is so pretty, if I were as pretty as her, I would be with somebody too.

Word of life: I am beautiful. God will bless me with options for marriage. She is not better than me, and I am not better than her. I am excellent in my way.

Your thought life has to be governed by the principles and concepts of God, or the world will influence it. The reason I can stay so calm when others are getting engaged is that I know God has not forgotten about me. He has written my name and your name in the palm of His hand. That is a truth that makes me happy.

> The battle with sexual integrity is won and lost in the mind. Refer to chapter 5 to revise how to guard your mind. And remember a righteous woman falls seven times and gets back up again.

DO NOT SWEAT THE SMALL STUFF

Now and then I have a sweat check moment. Something will happen that makes me stop and re-evaluate the priorities in my life. It could even be something on the TV or a news report of a sad event. It reminds me not to sweat the small stuff. I must let go of minor irritation and trivial problems that do not have a lasting impact on my life. When you put little things into perspective, it is not worth the emotional response. If someone is talking about me and I find out, I choose to let it go. If I misplace some money, I decide to let it go.

> [Mat 5:9 NKJV] 9 Blessed [are] the peacemakers, For they shall be called sons of God.

Life is best enjoyed when you are not at war with everything and everybody. I pity those women who are always ready to fight someone. So much anger, so much bitterness, makes their hearts black and awful. Ewel! Who wants to walk around with such ugliness? Let the stupid non-life-threatening stuff go. It is stealing joy and time from you. It is taking your happiness.

Conclusion

These are the weapons I use to thrive within singlehood. It is just normal for me now to be positive about my status in a genuine way. I do not need to mask bad days; I accept them as a part of the season. Looking over the last five years, God has purposefully taken me through a journey. Where are you in YOUR journey? Do you have joy in this season? I believe that when you are content with your life as is... it means you are at your dating best. This is quite beneficial when seeking to attract your future husband.

I want to encourage you that there is an opportunity to grow in this area of your life. Your singlehood season should not be prayed away. You should value each week of faith-building, self-discovery, purpose fulfilment and relational happiness with your loved ones. The key to your joy is not a husband, but it is your trust in God. You have not lost your faith that He will provide so you can relax because the promise is coming.

.

Chapter Eight

_____Singlehood_____

Whether you want to accept this or not, there is a singlehood crisis in the church today. The number of Christian Women with the desire for marriage and not getting married is increasing. There are not enough marriages taking place in the Kingdom. This bothers me, and it should worry every Christian in the UK as it is a direct breach of God's instruction… 'be fruitful and multiply' in the most literal sense.

A survey of over 7,000 adults (conducted by YouGov and analysed by David Pullinger, director of Single Friendly Church) uncovered some interesting statistics about men, women and the UK church in 2014.

They found out that: 'on average, across all Christian churches and denominations, half a million more women than men in the church. So it is indeed the case that gender ratios in the church are skewed –

and this is a particular problem for women seeking a spouse who shares their faith.' (10)

I believe the women to men ratio is as bad as 10 to 1 in many church locations. This means Church is not functioning as well as it could be. We are God's legal governing institution in the earth with many roles beyond congregational worship. We preach we disciple; we conduct outreach, we defend, we influence and primarily occupy in the planet (outside the four walls). However, when men are not present in their numbers... We lack. Men bring leadership and strength to the body of Christ. They have God-given place in the household of faith. We have simply come to accept the culture of a female majority institution which makes the Devil very happy.

This singlehood crisis is a multiple layered or multifaceted issue, whichever one you want. Here are some of the reasons I believe have contributed to our present situation.

Evangelism

I believe unmarried men are not in our Church because our evangelism drive is not what it should be. Evangelism is a job for all believers, but our programs are geared towards those inside the Church's four walls. It should not be left to those who are in the office of an evangelist or leader. The prevailing attitude of not wanting to share the good news with neighbours, friends, colleagues and strangers has contributed to the crisis. If men do not hear the gospel, they are unable to enter into the Kingdom. This is a failure on our behalf of not adequately carrying out the Great Commission given by our Saviour in Matthew 28. Therefore the number of potential spouses is impacted. Those who attend Church are usually married!

Church Splits

Church splits have done so much damage to the Kingdom of God. In some situations, the divisions are justified; in other cases to me, it was stupid. Leaders not wanting to serve under another and male egos have led to Kingdom casualties. The division has caused the natural networking of brothers and sisters in the faith to decrease. Some leaders go as far as to warn their members not to visit other churches. I heard that some Churches only allow their members to marry other members of that particular congregation.

Feminisation

A significant proportion of our western world Churches are not Men friendly. When men do get saved, they struggle to fit into the Church. Many Churches, not all, are not geared towards men. A friend pointed this out to me, and it made sense. The lovey dove feminine worship songs we sing, flowers everywhere, encouragement to hold hands all the time in prayer, female-dominated front line ministries, can be off-putting for a new male convert. My friend said: 'If the services are just about the emotional release if it is designed to distract and anaesthetise women to the hardships of life. If there is lots of sensitive display without substance... it is not going to attract men. Men need to be men. They need to lead in worship, actively build the Kingdom, solve problems, contend for the faith and hear sermons that galvanise them as the head of their households. They need to be taught and commissioned.

Youth drop out

A female-dominated environment could also explain why young men who used to attend with their parents, reach a certain age then choose to stay home. They decide to play sports on a day set aside for worship. The Church programs do not seem to minister to them. However, these sports are unable to nurture their soul or shape their minds towards righteousness. They do not ever reach a point of maturity in the Christian faith. The Jewish and Muslim cultures do not allow this. Their sons MUST attend their religious organisations as a matter of perception. To be honest, I think the presence of Fathers who take an active interest in their life makes a big difference.

Another point of haemorrhaging is when these young men go to University, they do not come back to their local Church. The emphasis appears to be on them establishing their careers, and marriage is not at the forefront of their mind. Faith takes a back seat to their innate desire to be settled financially.

Women's Retreat

'Some women may prefer to have fewer men in the Church because it is an environment where they can dominate.' My friend explains. Women may feel inferior or overlooked in other areas of their life. They feel safe and enjoy the power of ruling within Church with few men around.

Leadership

The last point my friend made was about leadership. It was a good conversation we had during the COVID 19 enforced lockdown. 'Some male leaders/pastors may enjoy being surrounded by a brigade of women.' Fewer men. Less competition.

One of the most diabolical things to happen to modern (ish) society was feminism. In the 1960s, there was a sudden rise in drug-taking, promotion of hedonistic lifestyles, the introduction of birth control and legal abortion. The Devil wanted people to think that premarital sex should carry no consequences. Men used to have to marry women to have sex as a norm. As a result, they would meet whatever standard was set, and marriage was respected. Women set the rule, but the cultural decision for women to 'get their needs met' to liberate themselves sexually has cost us stability. Wherever sex is easy to get, love, it becomes hard to find. What we see today is women having sex to secure a relationship. They compromise and give in as the norm, for fear of losing their 'good' man to another woman who will 'give it up.'

Church Culture

Okay so as we build this cake, let us add another layer which represents the cultural perspective and teaching of the traditional Pentecostal Church which I have

414

experience of. I believe cultural attitudes rather than scriptural wisdom regarding dating, love and marriage; this has adversely impacted peoples ability to socialise effectively. Many Women have adopted a passive approach in their love lives. Many are waiting on God to bring their perfect man to them through the church doors. Because this person is 'the one,' they will recognise each other at first glance, and the courtship will begin right after the first conversation. The only requisite is for them to love God and keep attending Church.

Now I do not want you to believe I am ignoring some beautiful testimonies. I think that God, in some instances, can supernaturally provide a spouse. When you hear some of these fantastic love stories, you can only attribute some of these match made in heaven connections with a divine undertone. However, we need to recognise when we are listening to an extraordinary story be mindful that it may be an exception... we may well be the rule. The same way that Jesus came through a virgin birth, that miracle was not repeated. An extreme example but please do understand my sentiment, which we have to learn about general scriptural principles, rather than just depending on the divine miracles in our social lives. If we were practising in our faith, then we would not need God to perform a miracle. He wants us to use the Word as a blueprint and make wise choices. He gave Noah the instructions, but He did not build the Ark. Noah had to be obedient. He uses his time and effort to put the vessel together. We are not taught correctly or effectively in singleness in most Churches.

Many Church cultures look down on the marriage desire of single people. Yes, some have made an idol out of 'love.' However, there is a mental attitude that your love for God must be compromised if you desire to have a spouse. They stand on the one scripture by Paul, in 1 Corinthians 6 where he encouraged single people to remain single so that they could serve God better. He highlighted how much more useful they could be to the Kingdom because they wouldn't be distracted by marriage.

On the other hand, this is only on the basis that their sexual desires are under control, and they understand Gods perfect will for their lives. Paul, I believe, felt Christ return was imminent... so there was no point in getting married because Jesus was coming back very soon. Can you imagine if everyone had listened to Paul and not married? They wouldn't be able to have families, and the bloodlines of Godly families would have stopped 100s of years later. Practically, it does make sense to be single as you only have to consider yourself in ministry. However, personal factors realistically MUST play a part in this decision. Being married may help someone serve God better.

Jesus taught that some were born Eunuchs as they do not have the desire for marriage. Others became eunuchs for the sake of the gospel. This, to me, is the gift of singleness everyone talks about, but it is given to people by God. It is supernatural empowerment because the biological proclivity of man is to procreate. It is not a default setting to have no sex drive or desire to have no children. Some seem to ignore the fact that marriage was God's idea and that it is an honourable thing to do. If you have the desire to marry, it is more than likely God's will for your life. The marriage joined by God will instruct you, and it will bring glory to the Kingdom of God. Marriage is for illustration, procreation and sanctification. Illustration because it shows the relationship between Christ and his bride the Church; procreation because we've got to be having babies and spreading Godly families all over this globe; and sanctification because it brings out the Christ in you. Marriage is a relationship which you need to mature if it is to be healthy and prosperous. It allows us to operate in the fullness and the definition of a real love found in 1st Corinthians chapter 13. Marriage is a good thing, and it is a God thing.

Generational Differences

My personal experience is steeped in Jamaican culture. When my grandparents' generation came to the UK and started the Church that I am now part of; they got married at a young age. There was limited career opportunities or equal access into specific industries that we as women now enjoy. So I feel that their understanding of the necessity of a dating process is limited. I believe in having elders to provide wisdom and objective guidance in learning about the character of a potential spouse. However, they are unlikely to have experienced singleness into their late 20s, 30s, 40s and 50's. So I am not surprised when older generations (65+) are closed-minded to dating agencies, online dating, dating multiple people and a longer courtship than six months. This is why I feel it is necessary to study singlehood, marriage and love in the Bible for yourself.

Let us go deeper.... The Christian community back in the day was a lot more closely knitted, and people grew up in very close geographical locations. Now we are all over the country. We are not attending the same two or three churches denominations. As a community of ethnic minority Christians, we are more dispersed, and I feel this has been one of the many contributing factors to the singlehood crisis that we now see in our Church. Some Churches remain as islands rather than different branches of this amazing organism called the Body of Christ. We are inundated with Christian events, and there is a semblance of being open to each other... but the truth beyond the social media campaigns is that we are divided.

Never-the-less, I believe my millennial generation is the key in bridging fellowships. Churches may have historically split for one reason of each other, but we millennials were not a part of it. We should carry the responsibility of cross-pollination for the sake of the Kingdom. There may not be potentials for you in your local Church or denomination body, but what about the other churches? Social media allows us to connect more comfortable with others, so why don't we do it? We also have to open our minds to different cultures. You may have a preference to marry someone with your cultural background, but what if your potential spouse is another culture but carries what you need. If we started breaking down cultural barriers and racial prejudice, we would accomplish much as the Church of God.

Observing the 'black culture,' another one of my learned friends speaks about the generational impact of slavery. I belong to this culture, so it is fascinating to me. He theorises that the proclivity of black men not to want to settle down or to have a lot of multiple sexual partners is related to their history as a people. Young men and Fathers were routinely separated from their families by slave owners and sold to another plantation to have children with other women. My ancestors in the Caribbean were treated like horses. Men were forced to have children with multiple women to produce more children to work as slaves.

Just as you can inherit physical illnesses, I believe you can inherit cultural mindsets, which can be positive or negative. The Bible is clear on the fact that after the Fall, we were born into sin and shaped in iniquity. I agree with my friend; I believe slavery provides some explanation for social patterns we note today in the 'black culture.' I am not suggesting that all men have this issue; I am just throwing something else out there for the sake of discourse.

I have oversimplified what a very complex issue is, but we can see it is not just the single people who are responsible for the current singlehood crisis. If we started to go into the attitudes of men towards marriage, we could debate and reason all day. I want you to appreciate that this singleness pandemic is very complicated. Sis, there is hope that God is going to address this injustice as marriage is on His heart.

> The Power the Change your Dating Life
> Lies With You

Singlehood Crisis Management

There is a beautiful book by a Christian psychologist Dr Henry Cloud, and it is titled 'How to get a date worth keeping.' (11) I think that this book is one of the most practical and insightful resources a single person can have. (Other than the Word of course!) He explains why we have to date and how to do it to increase our opportunities to get married. The Dating Coach service that I now offer utilises many of the principles he shares in the book, and I advise my clients to buy it.

I have noted the resistance by some of my clients, but the way I look at it is they have much to gain if they adopt a fresh approach to dating. I look at all the causes contributing to the lack of Christians marriages in the UK. We must focus on the reasons we can address ourselves.

Dating for Christians

Contrary to the widely held belief... dating is not just about finding the one! Sounds counter-productive, but this social activity is more than that. When the focus is only one particular outcome/destination (usually marriage), dating becomes pressuring! It becomes exhausting, especially when expectations are not met! It also becomes frustrating when you cannot seem to find the right one! I say, before actively dating... appreciate it for what it is.

Dating is about socialising with a man in a friendly manner which may lead to a romantic relationship. It is an opportunity to learn about yourself while you are getting to know someone else. You can use dating to identify excellent characteristics you would want in a future spouse. The person you choose to spend time with may or may not be your future spouse, but the time spent should be enjoyable and a valuable social experience.

Dating should not include sexual or emotional intimacy, and that is why you can date multiple people. It is a friendship you are building. In the eventuality that you discover someone, you see a future with, and they have expressed that they feel the same way... then it becomes appropriate to be exclusive. You move from dating to courting. The conversation becomes more intimate while you spend more quality time together in preparation for marriage. Emotional bonds are developed between you as time progresses.

Making friends with single Christian men who are new to you increases the likelihood of marriage. It is an opportunity to perfect the art of conversation, widen your world view, find out what your quirks are, overcome stereotypes you may hold and to be a blessing to others. All these things will develop attractive qualities in you.

Communication, respect and the ability to enjoy someone's company; contribute to building a foundation for marriage. Your date may not even be your type, but it creates the opportunity for a phenomenal love story.

When we go into dating scenarios already auditioning the person for the role of our spouse, we put invisible but tangible pressure on the interaction. Some of us become so nervous and worried about trying to impress them that we are not even ourselves. We also restrict the people we sit down and talk to in the first place because we think 'I would never marry him or her.' A lot of people who are happily married often end up with spouses that they did not expect. Their spouse was not their 'type.' You may get exactly who you want, but I encourage you not to box yourself in.

To date, we should set aside time to socialise. It means we must become better at managing our time. Being too busy to date implies that we are too busy in general. The fact that you hardly meet new single men means that your routine has become too rigid and predictable. If no one is approaching us or showing any romantic interest, it could be something we are doing to repel them.

It may feel uncomfortable to speak like this because we are so used to blaming God for not sending our spouse. The change in your dating life starts with you, and you must take responsibility for the things you can change.

[Pro 18:22 NKJV] 22 [He who] finds a wife finds a good [thing], And obtains favor from the LORD.

This verse was not meant for you to go into witness protection when it comes to men. It was not supposed to encourage you to become passive in socialising. It was not intended to absorb you of any responsibility in preparing for a husband. This proverb was to help men to be diligent in their search for a wife because she will bring great favour to his life. It was not meant to discourage you from looking out for a husband. We have misinterpreted and misapplied this proverb.

It has nothing to do with whether you start a conversation with a random dude or whether he starts a conversation with you.

A man can know you, have you in his life and not find a wife in you for himself. You could be best friends for years. You could have all the qualities of a suitable wife, but he does not want you. You could be that substitute girlfriend and he still not find a wife in you. This verse does not mean you need to hide away as in a game of hiding and seek. A lamp is set on a stand, so it gives light to the house. It would help if you were seen. Guarding in your heart is different from being seen. Just because you are accessible does not mean you are available to any guy. Learn to differentiate the two. Hiding your heart in Christ is different to isolating yourself in a social context. You may need to socially network to increase your opportunity of a Godly man 'finding' a wife in you.

Do you...

> Make eye contact and smile at men when out in public?

> Decline to go to birthday parties or events because you do not know anyone?

> Take time to dress attractively (not necessarily revealing) that shows you take pride in your appearance.

> Take time to invest in your health and grooming?

➢ Have hobbies/interests that bring you into contact with new people regularly?

➢ Always leave straight after a Church Service?

➢ Shy away from blind dates or online dating?

➢ Decline dates with men merely based on their appearance?

➢ Have a 'crush' and focus on him alone even though he has not expressed any interest in you?

➢ Complain that there are no good men 'out there' and give up on dating?

These are just some questions to make you review your current situation. If you are not happy with your dating life, then you have work to do. When you wanted to lose weight, God did not do it for you. You had to do the work of choosing a better diet and making time to exercise. When you wanted to get that qualification, God did not fill out the application form for you and send it off... you did it yourself. God puts the desire in your heart, but it is your responsibility to act on faith and take steps to make that desire a reality. Why is it any different in your dating life?

If you would like to get married, then take proactive steps to increase your chance of meeting your spouse. God can and will honour your faith. Even if He sends the perfect person your way, there are some things that you may need to work on, to make sure the relationship thrives—communicating effectively, healthy self-esteem, better time management, healthy sexuality and self-control. Dating helps with all of these personal development things. I suggest you get some accountability from mature and supportive friends. It is time to be intentional and does not put off tomorrow what can be done today. If you would like to see change... let it begin in you.

I want to revise our definition of Christian dating and courting because they are two different stages of a relationship. Please check out these summaries.

DATING

- Not for marriage but for social networking
- Freedom for multiple dates
- No physical intimacy
- No commitment expressed or expected
- Learning how to communicate
- Learning what you are looking for in a future spouse
- Enjoying conversation and getting to know someone
- Friendship focus

COURTING

- Spouse potential has been identified
- Exclusivity agreed between both of you
- Confirmation of a romantic relationship
- Deeper exploration of character and background
- Appropriate detailed conversation about future
- Marriage focus
- Discussion with accountability partners
- Openness with spiritual leaders ie Pastor

➢ Boundaries for physical intimacy (Affection based not sexual intimacy)

➢ Timing for progression of relationship agreed

Everyone always asks where the boundaries in showing affection are within courting. My advice is that instead of listing some 'rules,' because everyone is different, discuss it with your man. Purity is a direction of the heart, not just outward conformity to legalistic rules. Holding hands may be fine for one couple, but for another, it sends the guy into a frenzy. So you adapt to the more 'sensitive' partner. In general, making out, petting, taking naps together, massages... is playing with fire. Your body is engineered to 'get busy' so don't play with it!

I have to make a disclaimer that there is no one way to go about meeting your spouse and getting married. Instead, there are principles that you can apply that will hopefully protect you and direct you in making sensible decisions. God can and will oversee the process if you live a surrendered life to Him. At each step, you ask for His heart on the matter, and He will guide you. Not every social connection will be a long term or spouse potential, but you may learn something worthwhile. Enjoy the adult companionship and interaction for what it is.

Again I have to state that God may choose to make an exceptional circumstance out of you. He may indeed supernaturally manifest your spouse. I do not deny the miraculous meetings, visions, dreams, fast-paced, intense and authentic love stories. The issue I have is that a lot of women feel that they are in this category. The majority of you will not be though. Some experience miraculous healing, and there is a more significant number that has to use medicine to maintain their health. It could be about your level of faith but is more likely just the story that God has written for your life. Unless God confirms gives you specific instructions to do nothing; then I believe that it is wise to socialise with the opposite sex. Be practical. Be biblical. Be brave.

The final authority in your life is the Holy Spirit who will guide you. But do not blame God for your singleness if you have the desire to marry but have done nothing to prepare or position yourself. As we are talking about miracles, the majority of the healing stories demonstrated active partnership. Jesus gave them an instruction and the person receiving the miracle had to do something through faith to get it to manifest. To blind man, 'wash your eyes,' to the lame man 'take up your bed and walk,' taxes needed to be paid, 'go open up the fish's mouth,' and He said to the dead girl 'Talitha cumi.' Daughter arise! Sister arise. Proceed with caution, but my Lord does proceed. I believe being proactive is not 'helping' God, but it is showing Him that you are a faith walker, not just a talker. God will provide the prospects, and it is your job to be in a position to meet them.

Online Dating

Whether you want to believe it or not... online dating does work. You can meet attractive genuine people to befriend, and this connection may lead to marriage. I think Stanford University released a paper in 2019, which showed that just under 40% of marriages that took place in the preceding year met online. (12) As we become more submerged in the social media digital world... there is exposure to people you would not ordinarily meet in your routine life. I avoid the term 'real' life because many would argue that social media IS real. People are finding their dream jobs because a recruiter found them on 'Linkedin.' Online community groups that communicate on a specific cause lead you to interact with folks with the common interests.

Dating websites have exploded in popularity in the last ten years. Social platforms such as Facebook and Instagram have made it easier to direct/private message strangers. Meeting online is a way you can make new friends. Facts.

One would hope that you would apply the same common sense that you would to meeting a stranger on a train. So yes I would expect you to be guarding your sensitivity information like Address, finances, children's schools etc. But beyond basic common sense, I can reassure you that you need to apply a little more precaution when meeting online as it is easy for a con artists/faker to present false information as real. I used to do this when I was a young teenager. As a child, it was easy for me to put up a fake photo, I got a kick out of pretending, and I revelled in the attention. Others scammers may have a more sinister motivation. There are evil people everywhere. Protect yourself as a priority.

If you are even a bit interested in online dating, take time out to prepare yourself.

- ➤ What do I mens' first impression of me to be?
- ➤ Am I open to experiencing new positive connections?
- ➤ What can I work on when socialising with men?
- ➤ How will I protect my heart and my time?

➢ Other than marriage what the other benefits of networking?

Just like you have effective prayer, you can have an ineffective prayer. You cannot just 'do' online dating and declare it does not work after one month. But did you have goals? How did you approach it? Did you think about what pictures were going up? Did you design your bio? You need to have a positive and realistic mindset going into online dating. You should not feel you are entitled to lots of attention from mature men if your profile is not attractive. Men do not owe you anything. I feel... what you put in is what you get out. You have to be wise, cautious, yet friendly and open to conversation with positive people.

There are dating principles that I have developed over the years, and I would like to share them with you. I do enjoy teaching on this subject; my workshops are much more detailed. Keep up with my online itinerary to find out when and where the next session will be.

Manhandling, Myths, & Mudholes

DO	DONT
Please do a social media sweep. Check if he is on the internet anywhere else. Google their name. Most people have a digital footprint.	Please do not give him money or bank details. No matter what the sob story is or how long you have been speaking. It does not matter how he feels about you. Do not give out your money/ bank details. You are likely being conned.
Look through his social media platform. Most men will have one. Look for mutual friends. Look at what kind of content they share/post. It will show you their maturity level, interests and values.	Do not send him your pictures. Pre-select photos you like, a mixture of headshots and full-body within the last six months. Upload these pictures to instagram and redirect him there.
Look at the dates his pictures were posted. How old are they? Note whether they are professional or casual shots or their home. If all pictures are professional and look like they are out of a magazine... that is likely the case. Request more photos of them at home.	Do not agree to be in a relationship with a man you have not met in person. You should not allow yourself to become emotionally attached by speaking for weeks/months before meeting.

Request video call as soon as possible to verify the identity of the man you are speaking to. Facebook now offer this facility.	Limit the personal information you divulge in the first three months. Time is your friend. They must earn intimacy. Do not share your exact address, secrets, family business, medical history or financial information.
Get a cheap mobile as your date phone. Give out this number instead of your normal one.	Do not automatically ignore direct messages on your social media platforms. Check the senders' page first before you make a decision. If you determine that he is a nice guy. Send a polite message. There is no harm in providing a polite response.
When looking at his social media platforms, look at their comments. Is there a lady that is always commenting? Explore her page to see if there is a connection, especially photos with children. Some men are not upfront about their children, but the comments will highlight if the children pictured are his.	Do not assume that he is Christian even if this is noted on his page. Look for other evidence beyond a scripture quotation. Conversation, time and prayer will reveal the depth of his commitment.

When you decide to meet after a phone AND video call; meet in a public space. Carry money to cover your meal and transport home, if you have not driven. Tell someone where you are going and update them during the meeting. (bathroom etc)	Do not leave your drink or food unattended during a meet up. You do not know this person and whether they are capable of putting illicit substances in your beverages/food. Please do not get in their car or you theirs. Do not allow them to walk you to your car or home. Part ways and wait until they leave. Park in a well lit busy area. Do not go to each other home.
Meetup within weeks of speaking to confirm physical identity and determine if there is physical attraction.	Do not judge him solely on his photos. Request recent ones and also appreciate most heterosexual men do not know how to take flattering photos.
Ask them what they do for a living. Try to verify the facts. Eg if a lecturer, then they should be listed on the university website. Find them on linked in.	Do not change your social media to indicate you are speaking to a new man.

The points I raised above are barely scratching the surface, but it is an excellent foundation to build upon. The main thing is that you have to be patient. It is a case of numbers. When on dating sites you will be contacted by lots of 'undateables.' Lord, forgive me! Be patient with the process because different guys join up every week with a variety of motivation. Please do not get your hopes up for marriage but see it as social networking.

Disclaimer: I, Sara Jayne can not be take responsibility for your dating choices. I can advise on good practice but you must always be cautious.

Do not be discouraged when it feels that only 'undateables' are contacting you. Do not fall into the mental trap of feeling low and not worthy of attracting 'good' men. Sometimes guys, who know you are out of their league, will try their luck. They shoot their shot because they have nothing to lose. It is not a reflection of your value but just confirmation that you are attractive.

There are a lot of men who are seeking easy hooks up for sex, even on the so-called Christian dating websites. Do not be surprised by this. Anyways, be on guard for 'sex-craved sharks' and just know any man that suggest you compromise your purity standard is not a man God has provided for you. God will not want you to be with someone that leads you into sin. No matter how hard you pray, He will not bless a messy relationship like that.

The kind of site you join does make a difference. Free websites like Badoo, Plenty of Fish and CDFF, where you can message for free... are very popular. They are populated with guys who want more casual hooks up. Sites, where there is a membership fee, tend to be used by more serious guys. This is not a rule but an observation. Guys fishing for attention do not want to pay subscriptions as a preference. Sites like Eharmony, Match, Elite single have an increased choice of men who profess to be Christians.

Always confirm their marital status in the first conversation you have. You need to ask specific questions and never assume. Just because they have written something on their profile, it does not mean it is true. Some are hoping you fall in love with them quickly so when the truth comes out... you will not care. Ask them specifically: 'Are you married? Separated? Divorced?' Be very casual about it. If they are still married, they will say separated. Ask them when they separated? Are they legally separated? Are they still living in their home with their spouse?'

You will be surprised how many married men will put a single on their dating profile. You may also notice a pattern in their calls. Never early morning or late at night. They will speak to you on their way home but have to get off the phone when they reach. (They are going into their marital home). They prefer to text over a call. Video calling is not an option really at home. It can never be spontaneous. They do not want to give you a tour of their home. (Contains female decor/items). If you sense something, go with it and lock off the situation-ship. A lot of men consider themselves single even though they are not. As a woman who respects marriage... run. If he did to her, he would do it to you, no matter what he said the wife did. His character is deeply flawed, and he will not make a good spouse for you. Again, God will not give you someone else's husband. You may be in denial to believe that he will remain faithful to you. Adultery is a sin.

I can understand how easy it is to get into that situation, though. If the guy is a very good liar, you could be lured into a relationship without knowledge of a wife. By the time he tells you, or you find out, that emotional attachment can run deep. Even though you know it is the right thing to do, there is a tension in cutting him off. The 'what if' and the questions about whether you are 'the one' who completes him flood your mind. I empathise with the woman in this situation, but the right thing to do remains the right thing to do. You are worth more than sharing a man with another woman. Do not be anywhere near the reason that their relationship cannot reconcile. God is a fair judge, and how you treat marriage will come back to you. Run as fast as you can.

You cannot be friends with such a man. Block and delete because he will do everything in his power to remain connected to you. The longer you spend occupied with a man that is not yours, the longer you may be missing out on the real deal. Some men will not lie to you, but treat you like the queen you are. Your portion in life is not to be the other woman, but the only woman.

If a guy says that he is divorced, ask him when? And then when his final decree of divorce came through. When you ask these detailed questions, it leaves no room for ambiguity. He has to either lie or more often tell the truth. I have heard several excuses over the years. The papers have been filed but lost, or there is some sort of hold up. He will blame the wife usually, but the fact remains... he is not single. Although people think it's ok to date separated... I do not believe it is.

So... what TO look out for? What are the green flags? You should not ignore the nice guy. His page may be a little bland and pictures average. He may not dress the way you envision your future spouse dressing, but swag is something that is easily altered. You want someone who has not overwritten the profile. The essay writers are usually quite arrogant or self-conceited. Give them a wide berth. And on the flip side, a guy who has not bothered to fill out the profile at all is not worth conversation. Look at the level of education and their job, I am not giving you any rules, but what a guy does for living matters. A mature man will not feel settled or stable to build a home with a woman without consistent income. He may earn less, but he needs to contribute. I am wary of the mature student; I would like to explore what he has been doing in the earlier part of his life.

Respond to polite messages politely; kindness will not cost you anything. Give the 'average' guy a chance. He may not be your type, but dating is not just about finding a spouse but getting to know nice men. Learn from them and develop some friendships. If the flirt game is too strong, state that and express a desire for friendship.

I would not automatically ignore the shorter guy. Although, I have noticed some guys will lie about their height online or pretend they do not know. I do not understand why, because it is not something that they can keep secret, but they know most women prefer tall men. Give the shorter guys a chance; they can be very genuine men. They say short man syndrome is a real thing but try to network outside of your preference zone. If this shorter dude has everything else, you could want in a man... you would be insane to let him go because he is two inches shorter than your preference.

If he does not respond when you show interest in his profile, move on. Men go for what they are interested in. Take his non-response as an answer. Do not go back and check when he was last on. If an answer comes much later fine, but do not wait. You may not be his preference but trust me; this does not change your value.

On Facebook, make sure that you are demonstrating your personality with class. Do not overshare and show yourself in an embarrassing light. Do not like your crushes pictures two seconds after he posts them. Please refrain from liking every single photo, even the old ones. Do not be that stalker who comments on his every online activity. I am saying all of this because guys are turned off by desperation.

Make sure your profile is looking great. That means invest in decent photos. Every 3-6 months, update your photo. And yes, your profile photo should be of you. Takedown the flower or cross and show your beautiful face. Men are visual creatures, and they will not approach if they are not attracted to you. They will not come to find out what is in your heart when they do not know what your face looks like. This goes for dating apps as well. You need a good mixture of well lit good quality headshots WITHOUT the filters and full-lengths.

Do not be offended if men ask for more pictures. Just redirect them to your social media. Keep photos up to date. If you have put on some weight, use photographs that reflect that. If you have lost weight, update your pictures. Men want to avoid being cat-fished too. Do not mislead them with heavily edited photos or inaccurate body descriptions. Love yourself, show yourself and represent your brand of beauty. Trust me the right kind of men will be interested. If you lack self-confidence, then you will find dating more challenging.

You want to write enough in a dating profile to make readers want to find out more but not too much that they become bored. Be honest but not overly detailed. Be playful, witty and show your fun side. Write exciting things about what makes you unique and pleasant to be around. It is not a CV, so you do not need to oversell your qualifications and career. Men are not as interested in those things in the first instance. How do you relax? What was your most memorable holiday? Avoid stating what you do not want. No time wasters, no men with kids, no this and no that. All that does is make you seem contrary, and you are displaying all your insecurities upfront. It is not going to attract as many positive responses from the men you want to hear from.

I find humour helps throughout the profile but to be completely honest; your photos are the most significant factor in responses from men. Are things getting quiet? Update your pictures. Wear clothes that are flattering to your shape and suited for a nice dinner. If the outfit is too sexy, too much breast out, bikini, thigh exposure too high... they will assume sex is on the menu. I am sorry, but that is just the way it is. You want beautiful and flattering but leave some mystery. Nowadays, intrigue makes you stand out.

I am not going to give you an exact time frame when speaking on a dating app to provide the guy with your number for texting/calling etc. I will leave that up to your judgement. My block game is strong, so I do not mind giving my number out early on. I usually want to verify identity so a video call is organised soon after meeting a guy and establishing that I would like to know more. You do whatever is comfortable for you but if it has gone past a month or so... why? If you met a guy in the street or in a restaurant you would usually give your number at the time. Be cautious, but at some point, if you are interested... you should meet up as a next step before you decide to enter a relationship.

When you speak is essential. Late at night is not the best time to talk or connect. Both your guards will be down. He is likely to become inappropriate and sexually aroused. I am sorry again, but that is just the way it is. I do not care how 'saved' he is. Christian men are still biologically men, and to a certain extent, it is natural. It just needs to be managed, and mature men have a way of doing this. Help them out by putting boundaries in place to 'integrity proof' the conversation.

In late or early conversations morning avoid describing your nightwear. I would advise against doing video call in sexy nightclothes. This is just advice if you want to date the Christian way... in a manner that glorifies God. You may feel secure in your resolutions and purity, but there will be moments of weakness. Do not overestimate your strengths. Moments of loneliness strike especially at night, and it is incredible what you will tolerate. It feels good to the flesh, but it is poison to the spirit. Protect yourself. Even if you think you do, you do not know this man and you do not want guilt to mess up a potentially good connection.

Please, my dear sister, do not mistake intensity for integrity. Men have a gift for coming on super strong and passionate in the beginning. Conversations are deep, and they call often. But within one day, they can go from hot to cold. 'Ghosting' is a term to describe a man who suddenly stops communicating with a woman without warning; this is very common. If this happens, even if you think things were going well; do not chase up the man. Let him go. It may be something you said, but most likely, it is the man's choice.

His non-communication is all the closure you need. You do not need to know why. Let him go. If he is foolish enough to pass you up, it is his loss. You have not lost out. He has made room for another social connection that could potentially be the one for you. Make peace with the fact that he did not choose you; it is a freewill decision. Be assured of your worth; there is a greater man coming—smile on that promise. I believe that when they discover the level of favour and grace on your life, they compare themselves to it and may think they do not measure up. You may have communicated some reasonable non-negotiable standards that they know they cannot reach, and they are doing you a favour by eliminating themselves. This is why we guard our hearts, and every step of access has to be earned. If you have set boundaries in place to prevent premature emotional attachment or divulging secrets, their departure does not change your life one bit.

Sometimes guys 'ghost' because the conversation was monotonous. So I would suggest making sure you know how to be engaging. You can get work with a singlehood consultant from my agency or simply keep practising at home. E.g., instead of how was your day... you could ask when was the last time they cooked something for the first time. Speak about the exciting parts of your life and your hobbies. You want them to know you are an interesting person. I do think flirting is appropriate, but it should remain at playful banter and compliments which are not sexual. E.g. 'I appreciate a man who knows the way around the kitchen.'

As soon as you have met in person, relationship development becomes completely routine. You follow the same process as two people who met in 'real' life in the first place. Learn about them, do your due diligence and continue to ask meaningful questions.

Some people do not know where to start in the first meet up scenarios. So the last thing I am going to do in this segment is to share some first date questions:

- ➢ I really liked X... Y... or Z on your profile... tell me more about it?
- ➢ What attracted you to my profile in the first place?

➢ What is the last thing you heard that made you sad?

➢ What was the last good book you read?

➢ How would you describe your relationship with God?

➢ What is your funniest childhood memory?

➢ If you could only eat one thing for the rest of your life what would it be?

➢ How do you spend your spare time?

➢ How would you spend a million pounds?

Ask questions that are open not just yes or no. Also, prepare to answer the question yourself as they often will say 'what about you?' Actively listen to what the person is saying by being present in the moment giving visual/audio cues. Put your phone away out of respect, check it in the toilet. Chew like you have a secret and be polite to staff.

Please avoid asking questions about when they want to get married, future children, post-mortems on their relationships and your desires in these areas. It is too much pressure for a first meet up. In the first instance, you want to establish sanity and stability lol. There is a more appropriate time to bring up these topics.

I am a traditionalist so I believe men should pay for the first few dates at least. But sisters offer and thank them when they do cover the bill. Nothing throws cold water on a potential connection when you have to split the bill. I think about the fact that they did not budget for it. There is a chance that they may not want to see you again, even if nothing went wrong. I would advise you to bring money to cover your food but do not ever pay for his meal in this initial dating phase. He will take advantage of your kindness. I have been there too many times.

People ask me about progression and timelines. This varies from person to person, so I find it hard to set a hard and fast rule. Some men make their decision about their wives within the first few weeks. Others require three months, and some slowly catch on to the possibilities of a relationship after a year of friendship.

My advice would never assume, always ask if you are in doubt. In the dating stage, where there are multiple people you are conversing with, there is no progression beyond friendship.

If the guy does express interest after say a few weeks/ months, it is up to you now to make a decision. If it is too soon, please do express that concern. If the guy is serious, he will wait. If you have been 'talking' or dating for about three months, I would advise a conversation. I prefer when the men lead, as they know when they are ready. But after a certain point, for you to invest more time into the friendship, you should find out about his intentions. He may say he likes where things are going, and wants to continue. He may say I am interested in you, I like you, and I would like to be in a relationship (courting). Or he may say I am enjoying this friendship, but I do not see a future in it. Or he may not know at all. My warning would be to not invest your emotions and heart into a man who does not know. Keep your options open and guard your expectations.

> Your turn will come.

The Agency

In July 2019, I opened up a Christian Matchmaking agency that also offers singlehood support services. I understand why few people have done this... oh, my word it is challenging! The reason I opened up the agency was that I was not meeting any non-creepy single Christian men. My experience with online dating was frustrating and unfruitful until I changed my approach. I wanted to improve what is already out there in terms of networking for singles. I knew that the secret was uniting the different church groups... apart from evangelising to more men lol.

Although registration is online, everything else is offline. In this digital age, I am returning to personal service. My clients enjoy talking to a real person who wants to get to know them. You are not just a number, but you are treated as an individual. Christian single networking is such a niche market, and people need support navigating it.

I quickly realised that introducing single Christians to each other was not enough. I noticed a lot of my clients had 'interesting' approaches and perspectives about dating; it created obstacles in their pursuit of love. So I decided to offer Singlehood support and make that the central part of the VIP program. It is difficult for recruiting men, but we grow each month. God has used me to bring some couples together already, and it is worth every sweat drop. I have been inspired by the beautiful people that have come my way. I really do enjoy coaching and discipling people in singlehood. I am merely providing what I feel I needed.

I have an opportunity to work closely with some VIP clients, and the journey of evolution I witness is astounding. I see them growing in confidence and contentment. That is my number one goal. I always remind them that the priority is their emotional and spiritual well being. Whether or not we find their spouse during their membership period... they grow. They feel supported in their singlehood, and their hope for marriage is sustained. I challenge my clients where we discover areas of close-mindedness, immaturity, laziness or hardness. I help them talk through their concerns or insecurities in the dating process. We come up with Biblical pragmatic solutions together that they can implement.

Sometimes my clients just need a safe space to vent without fear of judgement. I encourage them when social connections do not go the way they wanted them to. I refocus them on the future that God holds so bright and full of promise. Where there is a history of addictions to porn/masturbation, I offer to help as a sponsor. I am a walking talking testimony that it is possible to be free. I also put on prayer meetings, webinars about makeup, fitness, online dating and collaborate with other singles ministry events. I want to rejuvenate the Single Adults Ministry in Churches across the UK.

I believe faith without works is dead. So if you have the faith for marriage, my agency will help with the works. I think my coaching can be summed up in three small actions that can produce mighty results:

➤ Pray effectively
➤ Prepare dutifully
➤ Position yourself strategically

The work that I do is time-consuming, but I see my time invested in people building the Kingdom. The Kingdom of God needs to expand through evangelism and marriages, bringing forth children. It is an honour to serve.

Benediction

It has taken me years to get to this point where I can say that I am addiction free, accomplished, experienced, matured and established, with a whole lot to offer my future husband. That is why I refuse to settle; I no longer cast my pearls before swine and let them get trampled on. If it were up to me, I would have written my story a little different, but it is not up to me. It is up to my loving Father, who is all-wise and worthy of trust. In this faith walk, He is in charge, and He is capable of blessing me with everything I need and mercifully bestowing on me all I want.

I do not need to go as far as to do a sologamy wedding ceremony, which I think is a bit loopy. But I feel freedom and comfort in knowing I am solely responsible for my happiness. It raises the bar, and the standard I have for my future husband helps guard my heart. His presence has to feel better than my peaceful solace. That is a tall order that only a man of God can fulfil.

Within these few pages, I have attempted to explore some of the issues single women face. I used my own stories to show you that even though I was hope broken, God healed me completely. My prayer was to help you restore your hope in love. It does work, but it starts with you loving God and loving yourself.

I do not want you to be manhandled, but to handle matters of the heart with wisdom and sensitivity. Accept that bad things can happen to good people, but the storms you encounter will not stop you from reaching your destiny. Your negative experiences are not indicators of your value. You are precious and will always be cherished in sight of your Father. He sent His Son to earth to die for you so that you can find your way to Him. That is why there is no lasting shame in making mistakes or bad decisions. You have not forfeited your destiny. Begin again. One step at a time and you will find that God will turn your mess into a message of hope for other women.

Hopefully, I have brought some clarity to the origin of some widely held thoughts about being a single Christian woman. This life is not necessarily towards you being a wife to a man here on earth; this life is all about being the bride of Christ. The pressure to get married is real, but God removes every burden put on your back. You are whole. You are special. You have a purpose. Do not let anything or anyone drive you off your track.

Come on out of any Mudhole you may have fallen into. It is not too deep or too impossible to escape. Do not remain in a bad situation because you are scared to be alone. That fear will go in Jesus name. That Mudhole is holding you back from experiencing real love. Let go.

There is no sexual sin that can keep you bound. Every addiction can be broken if you call upon the name of Jesus. He did it for me, and He will do it for you. You are not alone in this. I know it feels like people will judge you if you open your mouth. But exposing my struggle was a part of my healing. The blood of Jesus is strong enough to wash away every shred of sin. It will never lose its power. Come out of darkness into His marvellous light to experience what life is really about. Freedom is yours if you want it.

You are free to be entirely in love with God and still have a desire for marriage. The two need not compete. I am living proof that you can be content Single but also proactive in positioning yourself for marriage. Serving God is my priority, but it does not mean I am passive in my social life. I am enjoying this season of singleness because I chose it. I do not blame my circumstances or God. I am doing my part to put faith into action.

This meant changing my attitude, coming out of my comfort zone and being open to new positive social connections. I am excited about the future.

Mighty woman of God, God calls you because you are strong. Represent Him well. Love Him well. Heaven's resources are at your disposal to achieve your purpose. Walk single with your head held high. You will meet your Adam; he will be the RIGHT Man to bless your life. Do not look at what is behind you, or in your face but ignoring you, only look ahead.

Loudly, unashamedly make your footstep on this planet. Leave an indelible mark that lets the world know that you were here. This is your crucial assignment to take from this lesson.

And when you meet the man God wants for you, please send me the wedding pictures, so another sister will be encouraged that God is able. You can have it all.

THE END

References

1 http://www.oprah.com/inspiration/dr-phils-inspiring-advice-on-forgiveness_1
2 https://sanlab.psych.ucla.edu/wp-content/uploads/sites/31/2016/08/A-87.pdf
3 https://www.met.police.uk/advice/advice-and-information/rsa/rape-and-sexual-assault/how-to-report-rape-and-sexual-assault/
4 Gary R Collins, Christian Counseling, 2007

5 https://www.nationaldahelpline.org.uk/Contact-us
6 TD Jakes, Before You Do, 2008, TDJEnterprises

7 Williams, Kevin & Howell, Teresa & Cooper, Barry & Yuille, John & Paulhus, Delroy. (2009). Deviant Sexual Thoughts and Behaviors: The Roles of Personality and Pornography Use.
8 Philip Dada Jr, Saved but Bound Course Notes, 2019
9 https://blackandmarriedwithkids.com/2015/05/single-ladies-3-simple-ways-to-recognize-your-boaz-without-a-supernatural-sign/
10 David Pullinger, Single Friendly Church, YouGov, 2014
11 Dr Henry Cloud, How to get a date worth keeping, 2005
12 https://news.stanford.edu/2019/08/21/online-dating-popular-way-u-s-couples-meet/

Connect with Sara Jayne

Facebook: Adammeetevehere

Instagram: Adammeetevehere

Website: www.adammeetevehere.com

Send your feedback, reviews, messages, prayer requests and testimonies to:

admin@adammeetevehere.com